Activities in Self-Instructional Texts

Open and Distance Learning Series

Series Editor: Fred Lockwood

Exploring Open and Distance Learning Derek Rowntree

OPEN AND DISTANCE LEARNING SERIES

Activities in Self-Instructional Texts

NP

Nichols Publishing

KOGAN PAGE
Published in association with the
Institute of Educational Technology, Open University

First published in 1992

Kogan Page Limited
120 Pentonville Road
London N1 9JN

© Fred Lockwood, 1992

British Library Cataloguing in Publication Data

A CIP record for this book is available from the British Library

ISBN 0 7494 0709 3

Published in the USA by Nichols Publishing
P O Box 6036, East Brunswick, NJ 08816

A CIP record for this book is available from the Library of Congress

ISBN (US) 0 89397 379 3

Typeset by Koinonia Ltd, Bury
Printed and bound in Great Britain by Biddles Ltd, Guildford

Contents

List of activities, examples and figures

Activities

Examples

Figures

Series editor's foreword

The use of open and distance learning is increasing dramatically in all sections of education and training, both in the UK and around the world. Many schools, colleges, universities, companies and organizations are already using open and distance learning practices in their teaching and training and want to develop these further. Furthermore, many individuals have heard about open and distance learning and would welcome the opportunity to find out more about it and explore its potential.

Whatever your current interest in open and distance learning and experience within it, I believe there will be something in this series of short books for you. This series is directed at teachers, trainers, educational advisers, in-house training managers and training consultants involved in designing open and distance learning systems and materials. It will be invaluable for those working in learning environments ranging from industry and commerce to public sector organizations, from schools and colleges to universities.

This series is designed to provide a comprehensive coverage of the field of open and distance learning. Each title focuses on a different aspect of designing and developing open and distance learning and provides concrete advice and information, which is built upon current theory and research in the field and how it relates to actual practice. This basis, of theory, research and development experience, is unique in the area of open and distance learning. I say this with some confidence since the Open University Institute of Educational Technology, from which virtually all the authors are drawn, contains the largest collection of educational technologists (course designers, developers and researchers) in the world. Since the inception of the Open University in 1969 members of the Institute have made a major contribution to the design and production of learning systems and materials, not just in the Open University but in many other organizations in this country and elsewhere in the world. We would now like to share our experience and findings with you.

In this book, *Activities in Self-Instructional Texts*, I focus upon a characteristic of open and distance learning – the questions, exercises and activities that are an integral part of such texts. Throughout the book I have tried to do three things:

1. include a variety of examples from education and training – from the civil service to management, the catering industry to the leisure industry, primary schools to universities;
2. make the book interactive by giving you the opportunity to respond to activities in the text (the design of which I comment upon);
3. provide numerous quotes from both teachers and learners, so that you can compare these with your own views and those of your learners.

However, my main aim is to encourage you to look critically at the role of activities in your teaching and consider the implications of their inclusion for both you and your learners.

Fred Lockwood

Preface

In this Preface I want to put this book in context and give you an idea of what to expect in subsequent chapters. Of course, you might prefer to take a brief look at the contents and skim through the corresponding chapters and associated activities instead; this way may be more efficient.

The first thing I do in the Introduction is stress that the design of self-instructional material and provision of activities in teaching texts is not something new – even though the potential of self-instructional material has only received general recognition in the last 20 years or so. I then acknowledge the part played by those who developed linear and branching programmed learning and illustrate how these materials have contributed directly to the self-instructional materials that are currently produced.

The subsequent chapters represent the core of the book and give you the opportunity to explore how activities work, allow you to consider how research findings have contributed to our conception of activities and get you to consider both your own assumptions and expectations regarding activities as well as your learners' perceptions and use of them. The final chapter provides you with guidelines for the design of activities and encourages you to consider their implications for both you and your learners.

This isn't a typical textbook. It has numerous activities interspaced within the text that invite you to respond. It provides numerous examples drawn from a variety of subject areas and from a range of intellectual levels. Throughout you are invited to consider the implications of the arguments and illustrations for your teaching and for your learners.

Introduction

I have been surprised by how many teachers and trainers, lecturers and writers regard the provision of self-instructional material and inclusion of questions in the texts as something new and only appropriate to dedicated learners studying at advanced levels; it certainly isn't. Throughout the book I will be trying to illustrate the broad range of areas, and broad range of ability, in which self-instructional material is being successfully used. For example, if you have young children attending primary school ask them about the work cards they use in their lessons; I think you may be surprised by their variety and ingenuity. Example I.1, part of a sequence of material in a 16-page booklet which has been reduced from A4 size, is fairly typical of the self-correction exercises completed by 5 to 7-year-olds as they learn to use electronic calculators.

I suppose the dramatic growth in the Open University (OU) over the last 20 years has been partly responsible for any misconception since it has brought self-instructional material into the homes of many people and to the notice of many others. Certainly, with about 200,000 people currently studying with the OU and over 100,000 graduates in the country already, its influence has permeated virtually every school and factory, office and shop in the UK. In a similar way the Open Polytechnic, National Extension College and numerous correspondence colleges are bringing self-instructional material into the homes of mature learners.

Although the OU may have done much to raise the awareness of the general public about self-instructional material and its legitimacy, its methods owe much to those who developed programmed learning in the years following World War II. These teachers and trainers, who were greatly influenced by the psychologist B F Skinner and his model of the learning process based upon operant conditioning, attempted to lay out the sequence of a student's learning in precise, logical steps that resembled how a computer was programmed. In practice the teaching material was broken down into very small steps or segments (called frames) each of which

Example I.1 *Workcard for calculator practice* (Brighouse et al, 1987)

One is missing

Do these on your calculator.

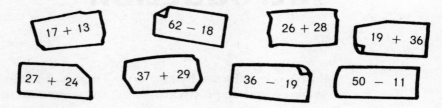

Find each answer on the grid.
Cover it with a counter.

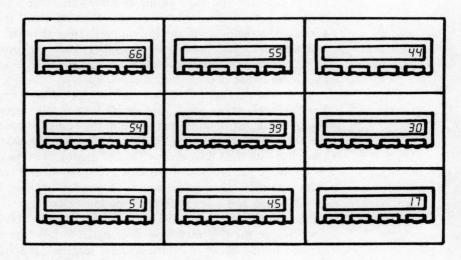

One answer has not been covered.
Write it here.

5

required a response from the learner before the programme could proceed to the next step in the sequence.

The simplest type of programmed learning materials were called *linear programmes* since the student would work through the whole sequence of steps or frames in a linear sequence. You may have actually come across some of these programmes in teaching machines – they were very common in the 1950s and 1960s. Some of them looked like a type of mechanical cash register which required the learner to press a lever corresponding to the required answer before the programme would allow the learner to proceed. Some looked like a television set that projected a still image or text onto the screen to which the learner had to respond by pressing the appropriate button. When these materials were designed it was common to build in devices to stop the learner inadvertently seeing the next frame or cheating. With mechanical devices it was easy to design a mechanism which would not allow the learner to see the next frame until a response had been made. In some cases the teaching machines required a learner to write in an answer on a paper scroll before they could roll the paper on to the next part of the programme.

In the 1950s and 1960s psychologists, military and industrial trainers reported widely upon the success of programmed learning in a whole range of learning contexts. It was obvious that if the benefits of programmed learning were to be made widely available either more machines would be needed or some other way devised by which to communicate these frames and record a response. It was found that, by asking the learner to use a piece of paper to mask the next frame, or arranging the text so that the page had to be turned to see the next frame, linear programmed texts could be published. It was later discovered that simple *student stoppers* (a row of symbols across the page) were sufficient to alert the learner to the end of the frame and the need to respond before continuing. In the 1960s and 1970s there was widespread interest in programmed texts and many were published. The extract from *A Programmed Introduction to STATISTICS*, shown in Example I.2, is typical. It arranged the statistical topics in a logical sequence, set out the teaching in great detail, listed the behavioural objectives that were to be achieved, and presented the teaching in a linear sequence of small steps. In fact I actually worked through Example I.2, which is part of a lesson consisting of 36 frames and a series of exercises, when I wanted to find out how to calculate a rank order correlation coefficient.

Linear programmed learning texts are fairly simple and straightforward to assemble. Unfortunately much teaching and learning doesn't follow a simple linear sequence, it follows a branching pattern. If you ask a question and an incorrect or inappropriate answer is given, you would probably

Example I.2 *Extract from a linear*

set 22

RANK ORDER CORRELATION

In each statistical technique presented so far, the researcher has had to assume that the raw scores were normally distributed in the population from which his sample or samples were selected. If he is unable to make this assumption he must use statistical techniques which do not require such an assumption. Thus, the Pearson product-moment correlation coefficient presented in Set 19 is an appropriate statistical technique for correlation analysis only when the scores in the population from which the samples have been drawn are normally distributed. If this assumption cannot be made, the use of the Pearson product-moment correlation technique is inappropriate, and the evaluation of its significance may be erroneous.

A correlation technique not concerned with the actual value of the raw scores or their distribution in the population is the *rank order correlation*. or *rho* (ρ). This is an appropriate statistical technique for determining the degree of correlation between two variables when you cannot make the assumption that they come from normally distributed populations. As will be discussed in this set, the rank order correlation does not take into account the value of the raw scores involved; it merely is concerned with the placement of each score in relation to the others in the distribution. This set will present methods for ranking scores and computing rank order correlation coefficients.

The method for evaluating the significance of the rank order correlation coefficient using Table 5 will be presented, as well as the basis upon which the null hypothesis is accepted or rejected.

SPECIFIC OBJECTIVES FOR SET 22

At the conclusion of this set you will be able to:

(1) rank order a set of scores.

(2) determine the ranks to be assigned to tied scores.

(3) use Formula 38 to calculate the rank order correlation coefficient (rho).

(4) use Table 5 to evaluate the significance of rho.

(5) identify the symbol ρ.

programmed learning textbook (Elzey, 1965)

1. If you have a set of scores on a variable that are arranged in order of magnitude, they are said to be *ranked*. Any set of scores can be _____.

ranked

2. If the largest score in a set of ten scores is assigned a rank of 1, the second largest score is assigned a rank of 2, and so on, then the smallest score is assigned a rank of ____.

10

3. The term *rank ordered* is used when you place the scores in order of magnitude and assign _____ to them.

ranks

Plate 90

Raw Scores	Ranks
47	1
39	2
38	3
35	4
31	5
29	6
27	7
N = 7	

4. This plate presents a set of scores that have been rank ordered. The first column presents the raw scores and the second presents their _____.

ranks

Example I.3 *Extract from a branching*

How detailed should you be in your description? Detailed enough to be sure the desired performance would be recognized by another competent person, and detailed enough so that others understand your intent as YOU understand it.

Here are some questions you can ask yourself about your objectives as a guide to your identifying important aspects of the target, or terminal, performances you wish to develop:

1. What will the learner be allowed to use?
2. What will the learner be denied?
3. Under what conditions will you expect the desired performance to occur?
4. Are there any skills that you are specifically NOT trying to develop? Does the objective exclude such skills?

To see if I have made myself clear, look at the objective below, and then turn to the page referred to under the part of the sentence you think tells something about the conditions under which the performance is to occur.

Given a list of factors leading to significant historical events,

page 53

be able to identify (underline) at least five factors contributing

page 55

to the Crash of 1929.

programmed learning textbook (Mager, 1990)

Conditions   53

You chose "given a list of factors leading to significant historical events" as the words describing the conditions or situation under which the selecting behavior was to occur.

Correct. These words tell you that students will not be expected to choose factors from a library of books or from an essay on history or from their memories. The statement tells them that a list will be provided and that they will be expected to recognize rather than to recall.

Here is another objective. Does it contain words describing the conditions under which the performance is to occur?

Given a list of thirty-five chemical elements, be able to recall (write) *the valences of at least thirty.*

Yes.   **Turn to page 57.**

No.   **Turn to page 58.**

Conditions   55

You said the phrase "be able to identify (*underline*)" describes conditions under which the identifying behavior would be expected to occur. Perhaps you are still thinking of the first characteristic of a useful objective, the one requiring the identification of a performance. If so, I'm glad you remembered it. But I am now asking for words that describe the situation or conditions under which the desired performance will be evaluated. Perhaps it will help if you ask the question "With what or to what is the learner doing whatever it is he or she is doing?"

Return to page 51, and select the other alternative.

want to resolve this error or misconception before proceeding. In a situation where several alternative answers are plausible, but only one acceptable, the selection of a plausible but inappropriate answer would need some immediate comment from you or direction to some remedial material before the learner progressed. If this starts to sound a bit involved and like a description of multiple choice question or objective tests – 'in response to the question below pick one answer from the four alternatives' – you are right. This method was the basis for *branching programmed learning* and stretched the capacity of both programme learning designers and teaching machines. In print form such branching programmed learning texts were published as 'scrambled' books. You started at the beginning of the book but were immediately directed, depending upon your answer to the questions posed, to other parts of it; you certainly couldn't read the book straight through. The printed branching programmed learning texts were extremely limited even though some have been remarkably successful and influential. Extracts from one scrambled book, *Preparing Instructional Objectives* by Robert Mager, shown in Example I.3, gives you an idea of the flavour of such books. (The original book was published in 1975, a revised second edition more recently.) The example illustrates three pages and indicates how the pages were scrambled.

I chose the Mager extract because his book, which emphasizes the specifying of instructional objectives, did much to influence programmed learning and subsequent self-instructional material produced by organizations like the OU. Indeed, the specification of objectives and developmental testing or field trial of draft texts before they are printed marked a significant point in the designing of self-instructional material.

So what has happened to programmed learning texts? Well, after the initial enthusiasm it was soon discovered that linear texts involved excessive and repetitive forms of response by the learners. The practice of breaking a topic of learning into minute segments from which the learner was virtually guaranteed the correct answer resulted in learners often becoming bored and feeling constrained. A regimented approach to learning didn't fit well into the conventional teaching or training environment. Furthermore, it proved to be extremely time-consuming and costly to produce. It is now quite rare to find either linear or branching programmed learning texts. However, developments in computer technology have given branching programmed learning material an extended life with continued interest in computer-assisted learning and computer-based training systems.

So what of the future of self-instructional texts? All the indicators suggest it is not just well but thriving, both in the UK and around the world. Everywhere I look I see evidence of self-instructional material being used – from high street banks and building societies to police forces and the armed services, from schools and colleges to insurance companies and industrial training centres. But the future is really in your hands. Whether you are involved in company training or teaching in further education, in a large institution or small department I trust there is much in this book for you. I would hope that after reading through the following chapters and responding to the various activities, your self-instructional material would be not just different but better. Certainly you would find it useful to have a collection of self-instructional material ready to hand as you work through *Activities in Self-Instructional Texts*.

Chapter 1

How do activities work?

A characteristic of self-instructional material

If you were to look through examples of self-instructional material from around the world you would notice that they possess one common characteristic: they all contain 'activities'. That is, they all pose questions in the text inviting the learner to respond in some way. If you doubt this claim you could check for yourself by having a look at a representative cross-secion of such material. I'm pretty sure you will be able to spot the activities – even if you can't understand exactly what they demand.

The activities posed in both national and international self-instructional material vary considerably in the model of teaching they adopt, their layout and design, the demands they make and the way they are flagged in the text. (In this chapter and later in the book we will consider these characteristics.) Furthermore, even within the English–speaking world these parts of the teaching material are identified by a variety of terms. In some contexts they are called 'self-assessment questions (SAQs)' in others, 'in-text questions (ITQs)'; there is even debate about the difference between SAQs and ITQs. The general terms 'exercise' or 'question' are also used. In the USA the terms 'adjunct aid', 'embedded question' and 'mathemagenic device' are often employed! Whilst the meaning of several of these terms is self-evident, the term 'mathemagenic device' may not be; if you are not familiar with it let me explain because it occurs frequently in the literature. The term was coined by Ernst Rothkopf; it

> … is derived from the Greek root *mathemain* – that which is learned – and *gignesthai* – to be born. Mathemagenic behaviours are behaviours that give birth to learning (Rothkopf, 1970, p 325).

I don't want to get bogged down in semantics and so have decided to use the term 'activity' to encompass all of the above wherever I can throughout this book. However, on occasions I do refer to some of the above terms when describing the work of particular individuals who have used terms other than 'activity'.

Assuming the truth of my claim, that activities are a universal feature of all self-instructional material, why is this so? Why do writers from different countries, organizations and cultures include them? I'd like to pose this question, this activity, to you and give you a few minutes to think about your reasons for including them – or why you may include them in your future writing. In Activity 1.1 I repeat the question, say why I think it is a worthwhile use of your time and offer a couple of sub-headings under which you can list your reasons. I have given you a couple of examples of possible reasons in case you are suddenly stuck! You can spend as much, or as little time as you think the question deserves. However, I suspect that two or three minutes would be sufficient to identify your main reasons. After Activity 1.1 I describe the reaction of others to whom I have posed this question and give examples of the reasons they have suggested for why activities are needed; you can compare your responses with theirs.

ACTIVITY 1.1 Why activities are needed in texts

Why do we need activities in self-instructional material? Their presence in material from all around the world, from the earliest stages of school to post-graduate level, from industrial to commercial training is not mere coincidence. The writers who devise them have sound pedagogic reasons for doing so.

Spend two to three minutes thinking why you feel they are needed in self-instructional material; the two sub-headings and examples below may help you.

To help students to:	To provide opportunities for learners to:
• think for themselves	• monitor their progress
• apply their learning	• check their understanding
•	•
•	•
•	•

When I have posed this question to other writers they have suggested that activities are needed to help learners to come up with their own explanation and solutions, to sort out the features of an argument, to draw inferences, to engage in controversy. Writers have remarked that activities provide opportunities for learners to be exposed to competing ideas and views, experience those tasks that are typical of the subject, practise important objectives, relate their own ideas and experience to the topic in question and to reflect on the implications of their learning.

In subsequent discussion a common belief, strongly held, was that activities were needed to encourage learners to actively use the material. Indeed, on several occasions the following quote, attributed to Confucius, was made:

What I hear I forget, what I see I remember, what I do I understand.

Three concepts influencing the design of activities

If there are good reasons for devising activities in self-instructional material the next obvious questions are: how do we devise them; what is the model or concept upon which their design is based? I would like to describe and illustrate three different concepts. The first, and one that has been extremely influential not only within the OU but around the world, is the concept of a *tutorial-in-print* (Rowntree, 1973). The second, termed *reflective action guide* (Rowntree, 1992) could be regarded as a development of the tutorial-in-print but has distinctive differences which have only recently been articulated. The third, *dialogue* (Evans and Nation, 1989a) is one that has attracted relatively little attention but one that I feel has considerable potential.

If you were expecting me to include models based on conventional textbooks or lecture plus notes you are going to be disappointed. I'm aware that most texts we learn from are not written in a self-instructional form. Indeed, some years ago a colleague published an article asking, 'Why can't a unit be more like a book?' (Jeffcote, 1981) – a unit being the self-instructional material the OU uses as the basis of its teaching. I'm also aware of the numerous attempts to make lecturing and explaining more effective (see Brown, 1978). However, I think these models are peripheral to the main points I want to raise in the context of self-instructional material.

Tutorial-in-print

At the time the first OU courses were in production an educational technologist within the OU (MacDonald-Ross, 1970) offered persuasive arguments for the integration of questions in OU teaching texts. MacDonald-Ross explained and illustrated the potential role questions in texts could play in encouraging an active response during students' study. Indeed, he recommended that 'Unit writing [the self-instructional material produced by OU writers] should not start before activities have been specified.' (MacDonald-Ross, 1970, p. 23).

A similar memo to OU course unit writers by a colleague (Rowntree, 1973) gave practical advice about the design of teaching material and originated the concept of a tutorial-in-print. The main idea behind the concept of a tutorial-in-print is deceptively simple. It starts by asking writers to imagine they have a learner in their company for several hours and to describe the *ideal* form of teaching that would take place if a topic of their choice were to be taught as effectively and as efficiently as possible; to simply consider what the teacher would be doing and what the learner would be expected to do during this time. Let me ask you. If you had a learner in your company for two hours, and wished to teach a topic, idea, skill or whatever, what would you do and what would you expect your learner to do?

Although I can't know what you would do, Rowntree argued that if you really were considering the *ideal* form of teaching it was highly unlikely that you would simply talk at the learner for hour after hour; he didn't believe it would happen. Instead he thought you would probably regard a one-to-one tutorial as an *ideal* form of teaching when information, source materials, procedures, techniques, arguments, research findings, raw data, etc. would be communicated and learners would be asked to respond to a variety of questions. In some cases the actual answer would be provided, in others a commentary or feedback. In such a context a learner could be asked a whole series of questions, dependent upon the nature of the topic and form the teaching was to take. The learner could be asked to recall items of information, to define concepts, draw together arguments, justify particular statements, consult other sources, interpret data, compare different interpretations of the same data, work out examples, discuss things and perhaps produce something themself. In short, teachers would expect the exercise of certain study skills by which the learner constructs his or her own picture of the subject and learns to integrate what has just been taught with what had been learnt before feedback was provided. Rowntree's tutorial-in-print is simply a simulation of this tutorial process, this *ideal* form of teaching, in print.

Within the OU the impact of his original memo and accompanying concept has been substantial. The questions in texts that Rowntree recommended, and the concept that he and his colleagues promoted within the Institute of Educational Technology (IET), has resulted in this becoming a characteristic of OU teaching material. Furthermore, the OU has promoted the concept both intentionally and unintentionally. When OU experience in the planning, production and evaluation of self-instructional materials was marketed as the course *Making Self-instructional Material for Adults* (Open University, 1985a) the concept of a tutorial-in-print was central to the planning and design and featured strongly in the advice it offered. The sale of these materials, supplemented by 10 days of associated workshops, has been extensive, on both a national and international basis. Furthermore, the success of the OU as a pioneer in teaching at a distance has led other national and overseas providers to regard its design of teaching materials as a model; activities in texts have become a feature of their teaching materials.

Although the concept of a tutorial-in-print was originally described in an internal OU memorandum (Rowntree, 1973) it has been reaffirmed in subsequent publications (Rowntree, 1974, 1979, 1985, 1990). For example, Rowntree commented:

> These tutorials-in-print simulate a dialogue between tutor and student, with frequent requests for the student to make a personal response and the author then continuing with a discussion of possible answers and where they might lead (Rowntree, 1974, p 119).

> This is why activities ... questions, tasks, exercises ... are a vital feature of self-instructional material ... to keep learners purposefully engaged with the material ... such a tutorial is an interaction between tutor and learner. This is what we are trying to simulate in the tutorial-in-print (Rowntree, 1990, p 120).

The effect of these implicit and explicit recommendations has been that authors have expended considerable time and effort on the design and production of activities and their integration into teaching texts and have placed considerable faith in their appropriateness for all students. Furthermore, the design of activities which are consistent with the concept of a tutorial-in-print need not be restricted to words within a specially printed study guide. Activities can contribute to learning in relation to, for example, newspapers, technical reports, video and audio recordings, periodicals and other published material, records, tapes and discs, experiments, tables, maps, charts and photographs.

For example, when the Police Central Planning Unit produced self-instructional material associated with the Road Traffic Act, 1991 (Central Planning Unit, 1991) their intention was to build upon their knowledge of the previous Road Traffic Act and to provide police officers with a 'working knowledge' of the new and amended legislation. The first page of the self-instructional material presented a photograph, an example of a typical incident and an activity (Example 1.1). Within the material a convention was adopted in which examples of road traffic incidents were placed within a boxed text and flagged with the letters E.G., the question(s) or activity posed flagged by an icon of a magnifying glass, quotes from the Road Traffic Act, 1991 signalled by an image of Big Ben and associated questions by a series of bold square bullets.

Police forces within the UK have drawn upon other media, such as audio and video materials, when designing activities within their self-instructional material. The West Midlands Police (Giles and Evans, 1991) have assembled a file of learning materials in which a criminal incident is simulated. The file, which explains and presents the case, contains the written notes of a police officer recording the original incident plus an audio tape recording of the interview between police officers and suspect. The activity, (Example 1.2) involves the compilation of a written record of the interview and completion of the official police form WC267; a critical part of the investigative procedure. You will note the typographical flagging of the activity, use of icons and space. Other police forces have used video tape in simulating realistic training. For example, Scottish officers (Scottish Police College and National Computing Centre, 1991) combined archive film and specially recorded video material to train officers in crowd control techniques and procedures. The award-winning training material (it won the ETTE Application Award, 1991) recreated the video surveillance images that would be available to different control stations at a large soccer match. The computer-controlled training material created crowd control problems, ranging from forged tickets to exploding tear gas canisters, and allowed officers to respond in extremely realistic, real-time conditions.

Of course, the use of electronic equipment may be completely unnecessary to present a worthwhile educational or training activity. It may require only a sheet of paper, pencil, scissors . . . and a bit of imagination. For example, after school children have viewed the various displays and studied materials associated with the principles of flight (Science Museum, 1991) they are encouraged to make their own paper 'Concorde' and conduct several simple experiments in controlling its flight. In the pages that precede the one presented as Example 1.3 the construction of the paper model is explained. The actual activity encourages pupils to experiment with different elevon positions, record their findings and to draw on previous teaching to explain what they see.

Example 1.1 *The Road Traffic Act, 1991* (Central Planning Unit, 1991)

CHAPTER 1: Serious Traffic Offences

We are now going to look at the new and amended offences created by the Road
Traffic Act 1991.

Imagine the following situation:

 E.G You are called to attend a fatal road traffic accident at 3.25 pm. On your arrival
you find the accident involves two vehicles, a car and a lorry. John Grayson has
been driving his car along a road in a built up area at speeds of 60 mph. He has
ignored red traffic lights and eventually collides with a lorry at a junction. Jane
Wood, who was driving the lorry, had pulled out from a side road. Mandy
Hobson, John's girlfriend, who was travelling in the front passenger seat of
John's car, has died as a result of the accident.

What offences are you thinking about?

'Death by reckless' may come to mind. In fact, sections 1 and 2 of the Road
Traffic Act (RTA) 1988 have been redrafted.

They now look like this:

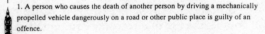 1. A person who causes the death of another person by driving a mechanically
propelled vehicle dangerously on a road or other public place is guilty of an
offence.

2. A person who drives a mechanically propelled vehicle dangerously on a road
or other public place is guilty of an offence.

I think that you would probably deal with this accident in the same way as you
previously have done. However, what the legislators have tried to do is make it
easier for the courts to convict drivers of these serious offences. Evidentially,
there are three things to consider now:

■ What is a mechanically propelled vehicle (MPV)?
■ What is meant by dangerously?
■ What is a road or other public place?

Example 1.2 *Record of tape recorded interviews* (Giles and Evans, 1991)

RECORD OF TAPE RECORDED INTERVIEWS

You should now feel familiar with the incident and be comfortable that you are the interviewing officer.

You are now going to listen to your interview and compile the written record of it. **REMEMBER** the points that have gone before, go back and refresh yourself if you need to.

 Now listen to the tape marked **INTERVIEW #1**- play it once to get the feel of the interview, and note down the tape time counter of any relevant points if you like.
The tape lasts about 15 minutes.

 Now listen to it again, and use the blank WC267 to make your record.

Example 1.3 *Effect of elevon position on flight* (Science Museum, 1991)

Fold back the paper or card along the lines so that you can hold the spine underneath the glider.
Stick the model together as shown.

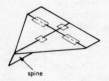

spine

The aircraft is called a delta glider because it is shaped like the Greek letter called delta (Δ).
Try launching the glider. It is likely that it will be too light at the front. Add a piece of Plasticine to the nose of the aircraft, making it easier for the glider to fly through the air. (Do not add too much or it will nose-dive.)

Controlling the flight of the glider

Delta planes like Concorde have elevons that serve as both ailerons and elevators. Make elevons by cutting slits 2 cm long in the positions shown.

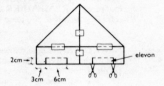

2cm — elevon
3cm 6cm

You should now be able to fold the elevons upwards or downwards along the dotted lines.
What happens when both elevons are raised or lowered?

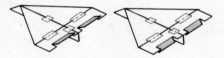

What happens when one elevon is raised while the other is level?
What happens when one is raised and the other is lowered?

Record what you see in a table like the one below.
Try to explain what you see.

Position of elevons		Observations
Right	**Left**	
level	level	
raised	raised	
lowered	lowered	
raised	level	
raised	lowered	

Example 1.4 *Assets and outgoings* (Inland Revenue, 1991)

2

3

4

In each of the following examples work out the amount of interest assessable on each spouse for 1991-92. Enter your workings and answers in the box opposite.

Example 2

Mrs Gilroy has a building society account in her own name. She marries on 6 July 1991 and puts the account in the joint names of herself and her husband on 30 November 1991. Interest was credited to the account as follows

	£
30 June 1991	500
31 December 1991	600

Example 3

Mr Barlow has a bank deposit account in his sole name. He marries on 5 October 1991. Interest was credited to the account as follows

	£
30 June 1991	250
31 December 1991	300

Example 4

Mr Webster, who held a building society account in his own name, marries on 5 June 1991. On 20 June 1991 he places the account in the joint names of himself and his wife. The following interest was credited to the account

	£
30 June 1991	150
31 December 1991	300

☐ Now check your answers with those on the next page

13

On many occasions all the materials needed to undertake the required activity may be available in print, as maps, charts, guidelines or tables. Certainly, when a tax inspector is calculating the joint assets and outgoings of my wife and myself for tax purposes he or she is guided by various factors in making the assessment. Trainee tax inspectors are engaged in a whole series of activities to ensure they are able to identify the appropriate rules and allowances so that they can apply them accurately. The self-instructional material designed by the Inland Revenue Open Learning Unit (Inland Revenue, 1991) identifies and explains the allowances, rules and procedures that must be applied; it even reproduces the actual forms inspectors will have to complete. Example 1.4 illustrates a typical revision quiz in which trainees apply the training they have been given.

It is not my intention to provide you with a working knowledge of the new and amended road traffic legislation, how to produce a written record of an interview, crowd control procedures, the effect of different elevon positions or income tax allowances – merely to illustrate how others are applying the concept of a tutorial-in-print to their teaching material. Whilst the above content is very specific the idea is common to many educational and training areas. I expect that if you were to obtain examples of self-instructional material from such different areas as accountancy and medicine, quantity surveying and geology you would find activities that draw upon printed or pictorial data in the text. Of course, an alternative is to apply the concept of a tutorial-in-print to material of your choice; Activity 1.2 does this.

ACTIVITY 1.2 Features of an activity (tutorial-in-print type) of your choice

Here's an opportunity for you to think about some aspect of your teaching or training and how you could draw upon the concept of a tutorial-in-print to start designing an activity for your material.

Imagine you have a learner with you for one hour to teach, explore, consider (or whatever) a topic that is part of a course of study; a topic you are familiar with. It can be anything from setting a broken bone to replacing disc pads on a motor car. If you could create the ideal learning context, offering the most effective and efficient teaching possible, what would you do and what would you get the learner to do?

I don't want you to list all the detailed questions, unless you want to, but to identify those experiences, events, resources . . . the components of the activity that would contribute to this learning experience.

You could, of course, spend hours on the task and end up with a whole array of documents, notes, resource materials etc. However, at this point I'd suggest you limit yourself to no more than five minutes – perhaps just jotting down key ideas.

I obviously can't know what your reaction to the above activity has been. If you are familiar with the concept of a tutorial-in-print, short of time, keen to get on to the section about the reflective action guide or more interested in my comments on the activity, you may have simply skipped it. If not, I hope you did spend a few minutes thinking about what you believe are the key learning experiences associated with that topic; the photographs, maps and charts, practical tasks, sights, sounds and smells, key questions and actions, etc. that constitute the ideal learning experience and which you could recreate in print. (The sounds and smells may be tricky, but with a bit of ingenuity I would be surprised if you couldn't devise something.)

The tutorial-in-print tries to simulate the personal tutor but in a situation where the tutor can predict fairly accurately the sort of response a learner is likely to make. It is most appropriate when the topic in question or the body of knowledge can be clearly identified. Rowntree has described this characteristic as follows:

> The tutorial-in-print style is perhaps most appropriate when there is a 'body of knowledge' to be mastered. Here the aim is to help the learner take on board a new way of looking at things. The writer sets frequent activities to ensure learners are keeping up with the argument. These activities focus on ideas and usually involve writing something down or tapping computer keys. The writer is able to give quite specific feedback because he or she knows the kind of thing that learners will have written. The learning is assumed to happen while the learner is interacting with the package (Rowntree, 1992, p 135).

The examples described above and presented in Examples 1.1 to 1.4 are of this type; they tend to dominate the activities that are included in self-instructional texts.

Reflective action guide

If I said that during a course of study much of the important learning could occur outside the self-instructional package, when a learner wasn't actually reading it, I suspect you would agree. If I said the greater proportion of study time to be devoted to a particular course may take place away from the teaching package you might still agree – but maybe less readily. If I said that during a course of study the nature of the actual activities would be so varied as to make it extremely difficult or even impossible to predict the outcome, I suspect you would begin to feel uneasy. However, this is the situation – where there isn't a clear body of knowledge to be mastered and where independent learning is encouraged – that is at the centre of the concept of the reflective action guide.

However, before elaborating upon the characteristics of the concept of a reflective action guide it is worth noting that the idea and practice certainly aren't new. Learners have long been equipped with the information and guidelines they need to engage in a learning task away from the classroom or textbook. I am sure you can think of examples where learners have been sent off to perform a whole variety of tasks ranging from scientific field work, collecting survey data via interviews, searching library archives ... to checking the engineering design, construction and appropriateness of a bridge of their choice. The practice is common in schools. For example, the GCSE geography syllabus (Midland Examining Group, 1990) includes field studies that take the learners out of the classroom and into the local community with direction and guidance from the teacher but little concrete help in conceiving, conducting and writing up the study – this is part of the learning activity and is assessed. The growth in such field studies and project-based learning is evident in self-instructional packages. The success of several OU projects within courses (Morgan, 1987) and even whole project courses (Open University, 1979a; 1982) are indicative of this growth. However, only recently has anyone made a clear distinction between those activities that relate to a known 'body of knowledge' and those that relate to 'one's own, unique situation': to the models of a tutorial-in-print and the reflective action guide respectively (Rowntree, 1992).

The concept of the reflective action guide is based upon several assumptions. A major one is that any activities within it merely offer advice and guidance to the learner's actions – actions in real and varied contexts, where some skill or ability is developed or refined, and where it is undertaken outside the confines of the printed text and which cannot be predicted. This could range from a farmer determining the balance of cereal crops, livestock and woodland for his or her own land to a walker deciding which route to take between Thirlmere and Ullswater in the Lake District. There are numerous routes between Thirlmere and Ullswater which may or may not include the peak of Helvellyn. The route would obviously depend upon the weather, time of day, ability and fitness of the walker, what the walker wanted to get out of the experience and so on. I chose the example of a walker because it is similar to the example that Rowntree gives in his discussion of the reflective action guide (Rowntree, 1992). He mentions the Lake District walking guides of AW Wainwright and how they offer different routes from which the reader can choose or from which they can make up their own.

A second feature of activities within a reflective action guide is that the learner must be involved in thinking critically, reflectively, upon his or her actions in order to guide the learning experience. It marks a major distinction between working within known parameters and setting them for oneself.

A third feature is that such activities are often demanding, time-consuming and relate to the unique situation in which the learner finds him or herself. While resources, guidelines and suggestions can be offered and drawn upon as and when needed, it is virtually impossible to provide feedback that would relate to the outcome of the activity in question. Learners need to gather and assess the feedback themselves.

Earlier I mentioned the field studies undertaken by pupils studying the GCSE geography course. Whilst field studies may not be a feature of GCSE home economics there is no shortage of illustrations of how an activity can involve a learner in a substantial amount of work away from the printed text with only a general idea of the likely outcome. For example, in a resource package for use in schools (The British Soft Drinks Association Limited, 1987), information related to the nutritional aspects of fruit juice is presented. Within one of the leaflets an activity is posed (Example 1.5) which would involve the pupil in menu planning, considering nutritional value, appearance, cost, etc.; a task including so many variables that a 'model answer' would be clearly impossible.

Examples of the reflective action guide can be found in a variety of other contexts, including many that exploit facilities, institutions and services that are readily available. When front-of-house operations (Thunhurst, 1990) were being described (these are the activities that take place in the reception areas of hotels or other institutions involved in providing accommodation or similar service; the sort of activity that receptionists perform) an activity was devised (Example 1.6) that sent the learner away from the printed material to investigate real front-of-house operations.

The activity in Example 1.6, in the box headed by three arrows and the words 'TO DO', invited learners to visit at least three establishments and from discussions with staff and information from brochures, find out what facilities and services they provide and what this tells one about the people who tend to use these services. While general guidelines can be provided, the nature of the activity prevents a model answer.

A similar activity, that sends the learner away from the self-instructional material and which involves collecting data and reflecting on it, was devised for sports coaches and their understanding of sporting injuries and appropriate treatment (Farrally, 1991). In this teaching situation the learner was encouraged to survey individuals who had sustained a muscle injury and to enquire about the treatment that was received and eventual recovery. The activity (Example 1.7) is flagged typographically, has an indication of the time to be devoted to it, provides clear instructions and a grid for the response and summary test.

Example 1.5 *Menu planning* (The British Soft Drinks Association Limited, 1987)

FRUIT JUICE

INTRODUCTION

The United Kingdom public have been steadily increasing their consumption of fruit juice over recent years. The annual growth rate for fruit juice drinking in the last five years was approximately ten per cent.

The table opposite compares the amount of fruit juice consumed per person per year in the UK and some other countries:

For many years it was customary for British Naval ships to carry a ration of lime or lemon juice as a protection against scurvy, a blood disease which was rampant aboard ship due to a vitamin C deficiency caused by a lack of fresh fruit and vegetables in the diet. The Merchant Shipping Act of 1867 finally made this compulsory for all British ships, which is how the British abroad acquired the nickname "limeys".

In the United Kingdom the consumption of fruit juice was traditionally limited to breakfast time with orange and grapefruit being the most popular flavours. Juices were also enjoyed as an alternative to alcohol in pubs.

ACTIVITY 1

Design a dinner menu for a tropical party, including a fruit juice punch.

Ensure when planning your menu that:

a) at least one of the main meal courses has fruit juice in the ingredients
b) it contains at least 15mg of vitamin C per portion
c) it can be prepared and cooked in 60 minutes
d) it is a desirable colour, flavour and texture

Is your meal healthy? If not, how could you improve it? Work out how much the meal costs.

The regular consumption of fruit juices as part of the daily diet developed in the mid to late-1970's. This growth was part of the general trend towards greater consumption of soft drinks as opposed to hot drinks and alcoholic drinks. The arrival of aseptic cartons, and particularly the 20cl size with straw attached,

FRUIT JUICE/NECTARS CONSUMPTION, LITRES FOR 1987

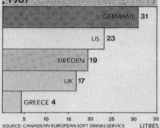

Country	Litres
GERMANY	31
US	23
SWEDEN	19
UK	17
GREECE	4

SOURCE: CANADEAN EUROPEAN SOFT DRINKS SERVICE

enabled fruit juice to be enjoyed anywhere and greatly increased consumption of fruit juices for refreshment.

Fruit juices as well as being drunk alone or in combination with other drinks — for example apple juice and ginger ale — are also used in the canning of fruit to replace sugar or saccharin syrup. Many recipes also involve using juices, such as beef in orange juice.

LEGISLATION

Control of fruit juices within the European Community is through an EEC Regulation which has been enacted in the UK as The Fruit Juices and Fruit Nectars Regulations 1977. This has set fruit juice standards and labelling requirements. The Food Labelling Regulations 1984 control the labelling of foodstuffs generally including fruit juice. Weights and measures regulations provide that almost all soft drink containers have to declare the average amount of the product in the pack. Food hygiene regulations ensure that these drinks are produced and served in hygienic conditions.

Fruit juice has to contain one hundred per cent juice with no peel, seeds or rag. Juice drinks, on the other hand, will always contain other ingredients as listed on the label.

Example 1.6 *Front-of-house operations* (Thunhurst, 1990)

 # THE CUSTOMER

Reception duties in premises offering overnight accommodation vary according to the type of establishment, how busy it is, and the needs of the guests. The mornings and early evenings, when most guests check in and out, tend to be the busiest and if the staff are able to work quickly and efficiently, the customers will be pleased with the quality of service.

Sometimes coach-loads of guests will check in at the same time. Where the establishment has shops, conference and leisure facilities, restaurants and bars, for example, there is likely to be a constant stream of people passing the reception desk and requiring attention.

What guests staying overnight want

What guests want will vary according to the type of establishment and the reasons they are staying there. Often the first contact potential guests have with reception staff is over the telephone, when they will ask whether the facilities they require are available, and at what price. A friendly and informative response from the receptionist could mean the difference between a room filled or a room left vacant.

◗ ◗ ◗ **TO DO**

From the following list choose and visit at least three establishments in your local area (as different as possible) and find out from brochures and by talking with reception staff what facilities and services each offers to overnight guests/residents. What do these services and facilities tell you about the type of people who use them?
hotels, motels, guesthouses, pubs
hospices
NHS and private hospitals
student halls of residence
condominiums, timeshares
holiday camps, theme parks
ships, ferries, trains, planes
NHS and private welfare homes
caravan parks
company training centres

What overnight guests may want

- room with en suite bathroom
- double, single or twin-bedded room
- bar open until the early hours
- breakfast in bed
- video films
- messages received and passed on
- trained staff available to look after children
- easy access to the room for infirm or wheelchair bound guest
- shoe cleaning, and clothes washing and ironing services or facilities

- room with a view
- orthopaedic bed
- meals available until late
- telephone, radio and television in the room
- clean, tidy room
- early morning call
- choice of continental or English breakfast
- tea and coffee making facilities in room
- choice of newspapers delivered to the room
- family room with cot and extra bed for a child

See videos *Guestcraft: A Good Reception* and *Customercraft: Keeping the Customers Satisfied*. More details of the organisation structure of hotels and the work of the different departments are given in *Working in the Hotel and Catering Industry*.

Tourist or resort hotels The guests will usually be on holiday and will want to relax and enjoy themselves. Many of these hotels have their own leisure facilities such as swimming pools and tennis courts. Friendly and relaxed service to suit the holiday mood does not mean a lower standard of service.

Motels or motor hotels They are mostly patronised by people on business travelling around the country by car. Some may be lonely and want to chat, others will want to get to their rooms as quickly as possible.

Transient hotels These are near a railway station, airport or sea port. Guests will check in and out at all hours of the day and night and may be on edge. Receptionists need to be skilful at avoiding situations which may cause tension and at checking guests out rapidly.

Residential hotels Catering for permanent residents and often called private hotels. A homely atmosphere may be required here.

Business hotels Used mostly by business people for overnight stays and for conferences and other business meetings. Quick and efficient service with good communication services such as telephones and fax machines may be what the customers require. Most establishments are situated in towns and cities where they are easily accessible.

Educational establishments Many universities and colleges provide

Example 1.7 *Muscle injuries and treatment* (Farrally, 1991)

ACTIVITY 8

For this activity, you need to talk to two or three people who have suffered recent muscle injuries. If you have been injured recently, you may use yourself as one of the examples.

i   *Find out exactly where in the muscle the injuries were sustained. Check to see if they occurred in different parts of the muscle (for example, some close to the ends of the muscle, others more in the middle)?*

SPORT	MUSCLE	LOCATION IN MUSCLE	RECOVERY TIME	TREATMENT RECEIVED

ii   *Find out if there was a difference in recovery time.*
Which location seemed to recover most quickly?
How does this relate to where most of the connective tissue lies in the muscle?

iii   *Your athletes may well have had physiotherapy, especially forms of heat treatment, to help them recover more quickly. Note whether or not they had treatment on the chart. Why should treatment be beneficial?*

iv   *Place a ring around the correct response:*

α *Muscle injuries which occur close to bone are likely to take longer to heal.*   *True/False*

α *Muscle injuries should be treated with ice when they first occur.*   *True/False*

α *Exercising a pulled muscle can speed up the recovery process.*   *True/False*

α *Keeping a muscle warm will speed up the recovery process.*

Example 1.8 *Training, promotion and reward systems* (Goodwin, 1991)

Let's now look at a current organisation that we are all familiar with, and see how it fits our Scientific Management model. When you have read the McDonalds case taken from Morgan's *Organisation Theory*, which is printed on the next page, tackle the activity which follows.

VISIT a local branch of McDonalds or talk to someone who works there to support your reading of the case study. (Failing this, WRITE to their Public Relations Department at 11-59 High Road London N2 8AW.) Ask them particularly about the **training, promotion** and **reward systems** that are in operation. Make notes on what you learn, then answer the questions below.

In what ways does the description of McDonalds fit our model of Scientific Management?

What evidence is there of working methods being determined by management?

What major role does the manager take?

How much scope does the local manager have for initiative?

What types of rewards are offered to employees?

▲▲▲

In what ways does the description of McDonalds fit our model of Scientific Management?

There are lots of examples: Standard procedures, even the use of automatic machines. Pre-determined work methods, a concentration on training. Even attempts to standardise speech – 'Is that a large one?' in response to a request for a drink. 'Would you like fries with that?' in response to a request for a main item of food. Managers giving instructions, staff following them religiously.

You have probably thought of others.

What evidence is there of working methods being determined by management?

The use of manuals and operative check lists. The fact that wherever you go you will get an identical product served in an identical way, by staff using identical 'scripts'.

What major role does the manager take?

Major decisions are obviously taken centrally, and the major role on site is the monitoring of performance – the product, the staff, adherence to procedures. Keeping costs, especially labour, within budgets, by careful scheduling of staff. Supplying central office with control information. Keeping the 'production line' working smoothly at all times. These roles are essentially 'technical' and 'administrative'.

How much scope does the local manager have for initiative?

Very little. Most aspects of the business are controlled by central office. They determine new products, advertising campaigns etc. The most freedom a manager would get would be in the choice of staff for the branch.

What types of rewards are offered to employees?

Mainly 'extrinsic' rewards – salary increases for longer service. Increased competency resulting in more badges, promotion to trainer and crew leader with salary increases.

The McDonalds case – conclusion

We can conclude therefore, that this is an excellent example of Scientific Management working well in a successful organisation. The two major drawbacks seem to be the lack of challenge to on site managers, and the mundane nature of work for operatives, which often manifests itself in very high labour turnover.

We will now look at some other writers on management approaches to see how they concentrated on other aspects of a manager's work.

We will look at the Classical Organisation Theory approach and also the Human Relations School.

READ pages 43 – 49 of *Management* by Baird et al.

▲▲▲

Although the features of activities with a reflective action guide can be identified, actual activities may incorporate features both of a reflective action guide and a tutorial-in-print. For example, when the Hotel Catering and Institutional Management Association was preparing its diploma level course in Operational Management: Food and Beverages (Goodwin, 1991) they asked learners to relate a scientific management model, that had been described previously, to a case study of McDonald's that was reprinted in the study material. The activity (Example 1.8) directed the learner away from the self-instructional material to their local McDonald's, and to reflect upon the extent to which this fast food outlet fitted the model of scientific management. However, unlike a major feature of the reflective action guide, the nature of the activity was such that the writer could anticipate the conclusions of the learner. Example 1.8, whilst containing all the typographical features that should now be becoming common, proceeded to offer comments on each of the questions posed.

In providing the above examples there was no intention of involving you with the actual content of them. As before, the intention was to illustrate how others are applying the concept of a reflective action guide to their teaching material. Activity 1.3 gives you an opportunity to consider how you could incorporate such an activity in your teaching.

ACTIVITY 1.3 Features of an activity (reflective action guide type) of your choice

Here's another opportunity for you to think about some aspect of your teaching or training, explore the concept of a reflective action guide and to start designing an activity for your material.

It may be more productive to briefly return to Activity 1.2 where you started to think through your ideas for an activity of the tutorial-in-print type. (In fact Activity 1.2 resembles the type that could be associated with a reflective action guide since the person who offered the guidelines and suggestions could have no idea of the actual outcome of the activity – the product(s) you would assemble.) Whatever the topic you selected, could an activity be designed that would take the learner outside the confines of the subject, so that field work of their choice was undertaken? Perhaps in thinking of the opportunities that are open to the learner you could identify those guidelines, suggestions and criteria against which to judge outcomes that would enable the learner to engage in the activity.

As with Activity 1.2, you could spend hours on the task and end up with a variety of ideas and suggestions. However, I'd suggest you limit yourself to no more than five minutes, perhaps just jotting down key ideas.

Dialogue

Some years ago an author argued that the more explanatory and clear the exposition, the less there was for the student to do; that some texts were so perfect as to stifle all real thinking. He maintained that:

> Although many are attractive, accurate, readable and understandable, they are also one of the biggest deterrents to thinking in the classroom, because writers assume that students learn best by studying a polished product. The key function of the writer is to explain, and a good explanation is interesting, orderly, accurate, and complete. The vocabulary suits the level of the student and complex ideas are clarified by dissection, integration, example and visual images. *Thus, the textbook is weak in that it offers little opportunity for any mental activity except remembering.* If there is an inference to be drawn, the author draws it, and if there is a significant relationship to be noted, the author points it out. There are no loose ends or incomplete analyses. The textbook is highly refined and as near perfection as a human mind is capable of making it – but the author does all the thinking. The book never gives a clue that the author pondered (maybe even agonized) over hundreds of decisions. The result is that the creative process and the controversy of competing ideas is hidden from the students (Sanders, 1966, p 158).

More recently, when expressing concern about the teaching methods that writers were employing in much self-instructional material, the limiting effect of many teaching texts was again identified. The writer remarked that:

> … I have seen some brilliantly articulated and beautifully illustrated course texts, but they especially can leave the student with a feeling of inadequacy in the face of such perfection, or (even worse) uncritical contentment with having been 'enlightened' (Evans, 1989, p 117).

Evans and fellow writer/researcher Daryl Nation have elaborated upon their concern and have argued strongly for a greater emphasis upon dialogue in self-instructional material. Their idea or concept of dialogue is not limited to the composition of the multi-media package and the place of activities – the 'instructional industrialism' or mechanical assembly of teaching texts that they have criticized (Evans and Nation, 1989b) but rather with the communication that the material generates and the reflective activities that they believe should permeate the whole teaching material. They suggest that dialogue should be regarded as a major feature of self-instructional material. In a recent article (Evans and Nation, 1989a) they review research and thinking in the field of distance education and argue strongly for students to be actively engaged in constructing meaning for themselves rather than being the mere receptacles of information supplied by the teacher. For Evans and Nation,

> ... dialogue involves the idea that humans in communication are engaged actively in the making and exchange of meanings, it is *not* merely about the *transmission* of messages (Evans and Nation, 1989a, p 37).

It involves sharing the thinking of the writer with the learner; to reproduce the form of communication that would take place between teacher and student as well as student and teacher during the process of learning. It does not assume a closed system where the boundaries of students' knowledge is set, questions posed and answers anticipated. It believes that learners, especially those studying self-instructional material, are the key persons responsible for their own learning. Indeed, the position that they adopt could be regarded as a further progression from tutorial-in-print, to reflective action guide to dialogue.

The suggestion that dialogue should permeate the whole teaching material has been accepted as a challenge by Evans, Nation and others who have illustrated how this can be achieved in the self-instructional material they have produced. Within the Masters degree in distance education, produced jointly by Deakin University, Victoria, and the University of South Australia, there are several examples of where the writer of the material has posed questions or presented statements that are designed to encourage the learner to pause and reflect critically upon the material. For example, in the introduction to *Critical Issues in Distance Education* (Evans, 1991) the writer presents his argument in a normal type face. He then shares his own thinking with the reader, and invites them to reflect on the points raised, by counterpoising material presented in italic print. Elsewhere within the course a three-way discussion of the actual concept of dialogue is represented as a transcript of the discussion between colleagues (Modra, 1991); whilst a dialogue between student, teacher and writer (Nunan, 1991) illustrates how other perspectives can be brought to the topic in question. Nunan represented the three perspectives by three different typefaces: serif for the writer, italic for the student and sans serif for the teacher. It is difficult to select an extract that gives the flavour of the dialogue since it develops over a number of pages; however, Example 1.9 is an extract from the end of dialogue which has all three perspectives, and typefaces, represented. Nation (1991) illustrated how dialogue may operate by including his personal thoughts in the text and putting these in brackets; see Example 1.10.

Although Evans and Nation regard the concept of dialogue as permeating the entire self-instructional text, it is worth noting the work of several writers and how their thinking and illustrations are influencing current practice with regard to the activities within this type of text. Writers who have tried to create a reflective and engaging text have invariably adopted a style of writing that is informal, using personal pronouns to create an informal or 'implied dialogue' (Gillard, 1981) that is sympathetic to the learner. However, other authors have gone further and have designed texts which require interrogation by the learner of both the materials and oneself (Reid, 1982) or have incorporated other 'invented readers' into the text who contribute to the printed dialogue (Mulkay, 1985). Below is an extract from the book written by Mulkay where he changes from a monologue into a dialogue and where he brings an independent voice into the text.

> I wish you were here with me now in my study, dear Reader, as I search for the words with which to introduce you to this volume. It would be much easier if we could *talk*, because in talking, I could answer any questions you wished to ask and provide an introduction designed specifically for you. One trouble with the printed word is that it commits you irrevocably to a particular sequence of words, when so many texts are always possible and so many are always needed… Unfortunately, I am condemned to rely on an introduction that takes the form of a written monologue … Of course, the written monologue does have some advantages … I will be able to make it quite clear that *this* is what the book is about. Yes, the written monologue confers a certain interpretive authority on its author. The more I think about it –
> *If you need me, why don't you invite me into the text?*
> Who said that ?
> *I did. If you want a dialogue instead of a monologue, why don't you invent a potential reader to talk to?*
> I can't do that. This is a serious academic study, not a fairy story (Mulkay, 1985, pp 1–2).

This may strike you as extremely novel and worth considering or merely a gimmick and to be avoided. However, I'm sure you would be interested to learn that there are examples around where writers have tried to reproduce a dialogue and to bring the reader into it and to include 'invented voices'. For example, when Rowntree was trying to explore the role of the educational technologist in teaching and training (Rowntree, 1990) he presented the transcript of a discussion between two educationalists and invited the reader into the text; see Example 1.11. There is certainly nothing new or 'trendy' about this as a method of teaching.

Example 1.9 *Dialogue between writer, student and teacher* (Nunan, 1991)

Of course, there is always the concern for directing the research activity in distance education to the real needs of the participants – those engaged in teaching at a distance, distance learners, and those who provide services and administer systems which deliver distance education. There is also the further question of whether any special characteristics of the enterprise of distance education shapes, limits, or promotes particular styles of research activity. I believe that my students should be familiar with the developing traditions of research activity within distance education and understand why research is directed towards certain problems. Equally, it is essential to connect research in distance education with the movements in research in education and the social sciences; students should not be constrained by boundaries imposed by current practitioners or researchers in distance education. Students should also be informed of possibilities, techniques and limitations of different, and sometimes competing, research discourses. This enables them to analyse, theorise, and pose questions which deal with a wealth of teaching and learning issues, macro-perspectives involving social and political effects, impacts of distance education systems, communication issues, and indeed, all of the richness of researching a complex entity.

I think I can leave the debate for now; I have the organising ideas of the area and enough background to be aware of possible criticisms, pitfalls, problems that can arise. What I need now is key resources in each of the three paradigms, as well as some signposts so that I can find my way down particular pathways in the paradigms.

Before we move to the next section, which covers the three paradigms, you may wish to read through the discussions. The discussion on 'Paradigms, ideologies and educational research' is to set the scene for introducing the paradigms; 'Linking theoretical constructs and observations' deals with the way that each paradigm considers the linking of constructs with observation; and 'The nature of research in distance education' considers the types of research activity undertaken in the field.

As well, as a teacher, I wish to acknowledge my debt to the teachers who made up the group that developed course materials to teach about research issues and methods. In writing the materials that follow I have drawn from their resources, discussions and approaches. The preceding story is an adaptation of some of the events that were part of the development of a book, *Issues and Methods of Research* by Helen Connole, Roger Wiseman, Bob Smith and Sandra Speedy. The paper by Ted Nunan in your text, *Research in Distance Education 1*, gives the actual story of the development.

Example 1.10 *Reflections on an introductory sociology course* (Nation, 1991)

In an introductory sociology course (Sociology 1) I taught recently, I used to begin with a discussion of two competing paradigms [that should send them to the dictionary] of teaching and learning. [Some of them will be aware of these. Some may even be converts!] I don't propose to rehearse that discussion here. If you are not familiar with it perhaps you could ask a fellow student, who has done that course for a lesson. [That should be enough to get the uninitiated enlightened; of course the old hands will learn more explaining to them than they ever did from me. That's why I am a magpie!]

[I'd better not leave the uninitiated completely out on a limb.] Without repeating the discussion in the Sociology 1 course, let me outline the two differing teaching styles which compete for attention in our schools. One can be seen as naturalistic, while the other is technological. The former regards teaching as something which occurs naturally in human interaction; as we do, we teach; as we participate in life, we can learn from our fellow humans and from other parts of nature. The latter regards teaching as a set of techniques; well developed strategies which put things in the sequences that empirical testing has shown to be necessary for effective learning to occur. Each of these is a model; in practice teachers tend to identify with one rather than the other, but to use bits of each.[I wonder if they can pick my own preference.]

You are probably asking yourself[I probably should have said:'may be asking yourself'], 'When is he going to get to the point? When are we going to find out about the specifics of these teaching methods?' Be patient! Anyway I can't stop you skipping ahead; this is print you know, and I'm not there [here?] in the room with you. You may be a student, but you are a free agent.

115

Example 1.11 *Teaching with conversation* (Rowntree, 1990)

they can 'get by' without developing their methods. What I'm suggesting, really, is that the educational technology approach involves not just using scientific *knowledge*. . . .

T: Which may be pretty thin on the ground?

E: All right. . . but also using scientific *method*. By that I mean a hypothesis-testing method.

T: Now how would you explain that?

E: Well, educational technology would want the teacher – the 'professional' teacher, as you called him – to think of himself as a tester of hypotheses about teaching and learning. That is, he'd start with hypotheses, insights, about what purposes might be worthwhile, or about possible ways of achieving the purposes. . .

T: From science?

How would **you** answer T's question about the source of the teacher's hypotheses ?

....

....

....

Now read on to see how E answered it.

E: Maybe from science, maybe from philosophy, maybe from his experience or from that of his colleagues, very often from the suggestions of his students. But quite often his hypotheses would seem to come right out of the blue. After all, there's nothing in science itself to generate new hypotheses. Even Einstein once said they came from 'intuition, resting on sympathetic experience'.

T: So you do allow for inspiration.

E: But of course. Inspiration, intuition, wisdom, good judgement. These underlie all innovation and growth in education. Science itself doesn't produce the new ideas.

T: Anyway, once you've got them . . .?

E: Yes, though scientific method doesn't produce the hypotheses, it does enable you to evaluate them and elaborate on them once you've got them.

T: I'm not sure I know what you mean by scientific method here.

How would you reply, as E, to T's remark ?

....

....

....

Now read E's reply.

E: Simply that you regard your hypotheses experimentally. You try them out with learners, expecting to find that they work with some and not with others, and to different degrees. You'll be trying to account for these differences, using whatever scientific or practical knowledge seems relevant. And you'll expect to modify your

Example 1.12 *Changes in financial management*
(National Association of Clinical Tutors, 1990)

1 Introduction

OPTION 2A

Resource management and clinical budgeting are permeating the NHS at great speed, but cannot be successfully introduced without good financial accounting. If your postgraduate centre (PGC) is anything like mine and countless others, you and your administrator will have found some difficulty filling in the sums for the core module to give you the real costs of running your PGC and its educational activities. This is due to the 'dual' funding of PGCs (DHA and trust funds) and to the way most DHAs lump running costs into district expenses under broad functional headings, e.g. cleaning, heating, telephone, salaries etc.

Most district finance departments are undergoing a revolution and it seems likely that PGCs will become an identified resource with a budget for all expenses and the clinical tutor as budget holder.

ACTIVITY 1
(allow about five minutes)

Changes in financial management

What do you think are the advantages and disadvantages of becoming a budget holder responsible for all your centre's income and expenses?

Advantages	*Disadvantages*
1	
2	
3	

You may feel it would be dull, too time consuming and that you are not qualified for the task. It would display your centre's assets for anyone to see and could lead to additional demands on your funds.

On the other hand it would give you the independence and freedom to manage the centre's staff and resources to get best value for money. With adequate support from accountant, treasurer and administrator all sharing out the tasks, the demands on your time can be contained and financial skills rapidly acquired.

If we don't get our accounting right and know where the money goes, it must damage our case for more funding.

More recently, when training materials were assembled by the National Association of Clinical Tutors (1990) the self-instructional material included activities of both the tutorial-in-print and reflective action guide type, as well as incorporating interjections from four 'invented' clinical tutors (the medical audience for whom the self-instructional training materials were designed). Within the textual material, 40 interjections designed to encourage reflection by the learners and foster dialogue were positioned (in bold italics) within the text; see Example 1.12. You will note from Example 1.12 that these 'invented voices', flagged by a corresponding pen line portrait sketch of the clinical tutor, complemented the more usual activity. It is also worth noting that while many of the interjections were drafted by writers, others were drawn from the feedback provided by developmental testers – clinical tutors who commented upon draft training material prior to it being finalized for printing. They attempt to raise other issues associated with the topic under discussion and provoke a reaction in the learner. Certainly, this technique of encouraging dialogue in the text by the inclusion of 'invented readers' need not be restricted to high level postgraduate training. Interjections in the text, flagged by a pen line sketch of the person commenting, have appeared in material designed for school children (South African Committee of Higher Education, 1988).

One way of deciding if the concept of dialogue is appropriate to your teaching and whether the inclusion of 'invented voices' could contribute to your material is to spend a bit of time thinking about it and even trying to draft some material. The final activity in this chapter provides this opportunity.

ACTIVITY 1.4 Features of an activity (dialogue / 'invented voice' type) of your choice

The concept of dialogue is one that permeates the whole teaching text; where the readers are continually invited to reflect on their learning, to construct meaning for themselves and where writer and learner share their thinking. The inclusion of 'invented voices' is merely a mechanism to facilitate this process.

Here is your opportunity to transform a small part of some existing material into dialogue and to invent one or more 'voices' of your own. The choice of material is obviously yours but, as before, it may be a more efficient use of your time if you return to Activities 1.2 and 1.3 where you started to develop your ideas for activities of the tutorial-in-print and reflective action guide type. The progression from the tutorial-in-print to reflective action guide and on to dialogue may be one you can accomplish with the ideas you have already considered.

As before, it would be possible for the task to take up hours of work, and the ideas associated with dialogue may be so appealing that it does. However, I'd suggest that you give yourself 10 minutes or so to create a dialogue for a small sample of material and decide how the invented voices would operate.

I obviously can't give you any feedback on your particular response to this activity. All I can do is ask you to consider whether the material really does encourage the learner to critically reflect on the ideas presented in the material. Does the sample material provide an opportunity for writer and learner to share their thinking, do the 'invented voices' promote this activity? If you are unsure you could try discussing the concept of dialogue with a friend or colleague, even asking their opinion on the sample material you have drafted and how they would react to it. In fact, as soon as you start doing this, and documenting it, you will be on the way to producing a dialogue for the topic in question!

Chapter 2

How influential is the research evidence?

Evidence to influence the design of activities

Let's assume that you are interested in designing effective and efficient activities for inclusion in your self-instructional material. Let me also assume that rather than just relying upon your own 'common sense' and accepted practice you are interested in what research evidence is available to inform your teaching. I obviously can't guess the precise research studies that have influenced your design of activities but we can identify some of the characteristics of research reported in the area, determine your preferences for particular styles or traditions of research, and then challenge some of the claims such research makes.

Experiments

Do you have a preference for a particular style or tradition of research and the way it is reported; one that you feel has the attributes of reliability and validity that must be at the centre of any research study? Would such a style be based on carefully controlled experiments, where subjects are carefully selected, allocated to experimental and control groups, and in which particular features (variables) are systematically investigated? Would it be a style that concentrates on measuring and predicting and where the entire experiment is amenable to replication for its verification? If so there are many research studies of this kind. Indeed, this sort of study dominates the research literature in the area of activities in texts. For example, experiments have been conducted on sample teaching texts where one version incorporates activities, a parallel version does not and subjects' learning on the two versions is assessed by a test. Such experiments have investigated a variety of variables such as the positioning of activities with respect to key information or methods of recording a response and typically quote statistical data and levels of significance.

This sort of experimental process is very similar to that practised in the natural sciences of physics and chemistry. It has been described as 'noumenal' (Marton and Svensson, 1979) and is characterized by researchers believing that what is to be measured during the research is already known. It is merely a case of quantifying it. Would evidence of this type influence you in the way you design and present activities in texts?

Qualitative studies

What about a completely different style of research or tradition? Would it be one where instead of selecting the variables to be researched and carefully controlling them, the emphasis would be upon exploring an aspect of learning and understanding how learning takes place, perhaps where learners' responses in a small number of interviews and discussions shape and direct the research? There is a small but growing amount of qualitative research of this type being reported which typically progresses from a broad range of topics and potential lines of enquiry to a concentration upon those issues that emerge which are of significant importance to learners and thus to writers. Often such research is involved in developing the theoretical constructs which explain how students learn. For example, qualitative studies have revealed that it is relatively easy to induce surface level processing of a text (typified by concentrating on superficial and intellectually low level activities) but that attempts to promote deep level processing (where an understanding of the principles, ideas and relationships is involved) can result in a learner's response being 'technified' (a phrase that has been coined to describe how answers are formulated to anticipated questions rather than to the principles, ideas and relationships that underlie it) (Marton and Säljö, 1976). Similar qualitative studies have revealed the strategies that learners adopt when anticipating questions – strategies that can be counter-productive.

The sort of evidence collected from this qualitative research is similar to that used in the social sciences. It has been termed 'phenomenal' (Marton and Säljö, 1976) where the focus is upon the quality of student learning, what they understand, the context in which learning takes place and their awareness of their own learning. Would evidence of this type influence you in the way you design and present your activities?

Surveys

If you feel these two styles of research represent extremes, sometimes described in terms of a structured-unstructured continuum, perhaps you would be more receptive to one that sits between them. If so perhaps it would be based upon survey techniques which can range from exploratory interviews to standardized questionnaires; techniques in which particular issues are investigated via closed-ended and open-ended questions with a carefully selected sample of learners. The resultant data are often analysed statistically with subsequent interpretations identifying any trends and their statistical significance. It may involve qualitative analyses which seek to identify and explain emergent issues. Certainly many researchers regard this style of research as appropriate to a wide range of enquiries. Furthermore, such research can be extremely cheap compared to other methods like experiments and interviews. Large numbers can be involved and one is able to focus on specific issues and responses to key questions by either having learners select from a choice of alternative answers (closed-ended responses) or provide their own in response to questionnaire items (open-ended responses).

Research studies of this type are extremely common. They have revealed learners' concern over the time consumed by activities, how providing a space or framework for a response influences the likelihood of a response and reaction when activities are omitted from the teaching text. Would evidence from surveys be that which would influence your design of activities?

Your preferences

The above descriptions and comments serve to highlight three different styles or traditions of research. Of course, researchers do not slavishly work within one style or tradition irrespective of the problem they are investigating. Conducting an experiment, adopting a qualitative style of research or conducting a survey is not simply good or bad but preferable for some tasks, under some conditions and not in others. However, as a preliminary to a consideration of those research findings that have dominated thinking with regard to activities, I think it would be worthwhile to consider your preferences for particular styles or traditions of research in Activity 2.1 below.

ACTIVITY 2.1 Preferences for different styles of research

Below I have listed a series of features of reported research which are often regarded as indicators of its legitimacy and worth. I'd like you to read through each of them in turn and, in light of the above comments, tick those you feel would be likely to influence you in designing activities in your teaching material. The exercise could alert you to the preferences you have and the 'evidence' you draw upon to support your current practice.

		tick those that apply
1.	Emphasis on measurement and prediction of variables	( )
2.	Based on interviews and small group discussions	( )
3.	Learners who participate are carefully selected	( )
4.	Nature of the research study makes it easy to replicate	( )
5.	Analysis employs statistical procedures and techniques	( )
6.	Conduct of the study and findings must be valid	( )
7.	Eventual focus of the study emerges during the research	( )
8.	Findings contribute to theory building	( )
9.	Confidence supported by large scale data collection	( )
10.	Any possible bias in the data collected reduced to a minimum	( )
11.	Involves systematic control of all key variables	( )
12.	Emphasis on description and understanding of what is happening	( )

Speculating upon which features you have ticked, and whether there is any pattern in your choice, is difficult. However, I suspect that virtually everyone will have ticked 6 and 8, since if the findings are not valid one can have no confidence in them at all and if the research tasks conducted do not make a contribution to theory building, no matter how small, they merely represent isolated, descriptive accounts.

I also suspect that many will have ticked 3, 4, and 10 and that some will prefer features associated with experiments while others prefer those associated with qualitative research. However, with regard to any possible division, as typified by the grouped features 1, 5, 9 and 11 and by 2, 7 and 12, I would like to suggest that association of the above features may not be restricted to a single style or tradition of research.

In terms of the list of features in Activity 2.1, my guess is that many will have ticked 3, since this is a feature of all research. Those conducting experiments may wish to identify particular population characteristics, distribute these at random throughout the groups or allocate them to experimental and control groups as a way of systematically controlling variables. Similarly, sample selection is a major concern of survey research if statistical controls are to be applied and if generalizations are to be made to the wider population. Indeed, there is an entire research literature associated with different forms of sampling and their implications for subsequent analysis and interpretation (Moser, 1971). The choice of participants in interviews is equally important. Indeed, in certain forms of qualitative study researchers speak of their 'informants' (Geotz, 1984); typically individuals with a particular position in a group or characteristics that make their comments invaluable. In other studies the generalizability of the findings may be a goal which would be dependent upon the participants' representativeness of a wider population.

Item 4 is also likely to be ticked by many. If your initial reaction is that it is only experiments and surveys that can be replicated, think again. It is certainly true that experiments and surveys, with clearly specified conditions, carefully controlled variables and documented materials, are most amenable to replication. However, qualitative studies typically display reflexivity – a clear and detailed account of how the study was conducted, findings obtained and how these findings were analysed and interpreted. A detailed description of the ideas, concepts or relationships that emerged, together with illustrations and links to other research and theories are common features. It is thus possible for other researchers to explore the same area and to either confirm or refute the findings that were obtained. It is even possible for other researchers to re-analyse the original data assembled and offer similar or alternative interpretations. Whilst this isn't replication in the strictest sense of the term it is an indicator of reliability. For example, a Swedish researcher displayed reflexivity in his account of how individual learners respond to learning tasks in different ways because they have different conceptions of what learning involves. He suggested that these different conceptions of learning dictate how individuals perceive and subsequently undertake the task of studying (Säljö, 1979a). His reflexive account enabled researchers within the Open University (Morgan et al, 1981) to conduct similar studies and support his findings.

Item 10 is also likely to be ticked by many. The aim in all research is to eliminate systematic error in any data that are collected; recognizing and reducing the effect of the experimenter, surveyor and interviewer are activities common to all styles and traditions of research. In experiments, for example, it is common to institute double-blind procedures (a procedure that keeps information about the design of the experiment confidential so that the experimenter does not know the significance of the different groups and treatments). Surveyors are aware, for example, that the actual phrasing of questionnaire items, sequences of yes/no answers, venue and time of day for conducting the survey have been shown to influence responses. In other research contexts the age, sex, colour, dress and accent of interviewers have also been shown to result in systematic bias; this is apart from any idiosyncratic bias that the individual brings to the research study.

I hope Activity 2.1 and the associated comments have helped you to decide whether you have a preference for a particular research style or not.

I also hope the above comments have alerted you to some of the features that are likely to be central to any account of reported research. With this as a basis we can now consider some of the features of experimental research – research which has dominated thinking in the design of activities in texts for many years.

Generalizability of experimental findings to self-instructional texts

There is an enormous literature on the effect of questions in texts upon student learning. The majority of it is dominated by the experimental studies of Rothkopf and his colleagues and his concept of 'mathemagenic behaviour'. It is based on the hypothesis that readers who are presented with questions will begin to process the text more thoroughly in order to be able to answer subsequent questions. The conclusion which is generally drawn from the literature is that such devices improve learning outcomes. The initial study (Rothkopf, 1965) and much subsequent research has produced a fair consensus concerning the effects of inserted questions, summarized below:

1. Inserted questions which appear before the material to which they relate (pre-questions) have a substantial specific facilitative effect but no general facilitative effect.
2. Inserted questions which appear after the material to which they relate (post-question) have a substantial specific facilitative effect as well as a small general facilitative effect on post-test scores.

That is, both pre-questions and post-questions facilitate intentional learning, but only post-questions facilitate incidental learning (Faw and Waller, 1976, p 700).

This consensus which has emerged from literally hundreds of separate investigations, enquiries and research exercises, is not in doubt. However, many researchers are increasingly challenging the generalizability of the findings to normal study.

In Activity 2.2 I'd like to provide you with an opportunity to read through the actual published description of a real experiment and form your own judgement.

ACTIVITY 2.2   A published account of some experimental research

The abstract of the published paper is reproduced below; it will give you an overview of the experimental study. The symbol χ indicates the arithmetic mean or average score.

Can delivery of adjunct questions by teachers promote more effective study of written material than written adjunct questions embedded in text? High school students (N=63) studied a 16,000 word earth science text presented on 108 slides. Treatments were: written question, one written question every sixth slide; oral question, one question asked by a teacher orally every sixth slide; and a control group without adjunct questions. The oral question group scored significantly higher on a criterion test (χ = 56.0%) than the written question group (χ = 48.8%). Both groups scored significantly higher than the control (χ = 42.8%).

The material used in the experiment was drawn from four chapters of an earth science textbook which dealt with rivers, glaciers and the geological features produced by them. The 16,000 words were typed on 108 pages (of between 100–200 words per page) and reproduced as 35mm photographic slides. The extract below, from the published paper, indicates how the apparatus was set up.

Each subject was seated in a wooden portable booth that shielded him visually from other subjects and from the experimenter station. The booth contained a shelf table. Centred on this shelf and mounted vertically about eye height in the wall of the booth faced by the subject was a 50.8 x 38.1 centimetre rear projection screen made of rigid plastic (Polacoat LS75PL). The text materials were projected onto this screen by use of a Kodak Carousel slide projector equipped with a 3.554 centimetre lens. The slide projector was mounted on a shelf outside of the booth with the focal plane of the projector approximately 48.6 centimetres to the rear of the projection screen.

The projector was operated by a switch on the table inside the subject's booth. When the subject pressed the switch the following sequence of events took place: (a) a solenoid-operated shutter occluded the optical path; (b) the slide tray of the projector advanced by one; and (c) the shutter reopened revealing the next slide on the screen.

The experimenter was able to monitor the progress of three subjects at a time by means of an automatic counter attached to the slide projector and to record the time spent on each slide. The following extract indicates the actual experimental procedures that were followed.

Subjects entered the experimental room individually. After initial directions, they were seated in their booths, and the slide reading apparatus was explained to them. Three subjects were run at one time. Each group of three subjects was assigned in an unbiased manner to one of three experimental conditions. Regardless of treatment assignment, the subjects read the first 24 text slides without exposure to any questions and without further contact with the experimenter. In the written question treatment, one written question was included in the slide sequence after every sixth text slide in the sequence between text slides 25 and 108. The question was always relevant to material in one of the six preceding text slides. In the written question treatment, the subjects were directed to write the answer to each question on a slip on paper, and to insert the answer slip in a ballot box located within the booth. No knowledge of results was provided.

In the second treatment, oral questions, the questions were the same as those used in the written question treatment and they were asked in the same places in the text sequence. However, in the oral question condition, the monitor (experimenter) asked the question. This was done in the following way.

The paper proceeded to describe in detail how the mechanism worked and how the experimenter was prompted to pose a verbal question.

The questions were spoken in a low, well intoned, but relatively neutral voice. During questioning, the experimenter stood behind the subject's right shoulder. Normally there was no eye contact between the experimenter and the subject. However, the experimenter did not systematically attempt to avoid such contact. If the subject paused after the question was read, it was repeated once. After the subject had responded, the experimenter left the booth without providing any feedback. The total contact time for each question event lasted from 10 to 40 seconds depending on how quickly the subject responded to the question.

No questions were asked of the subjects in the third question treatment. Those assigned to this treatment read text slides 25–108 under the same condition that they read slides 1–24.

After the first 66 text slides had been inspected, each subject left the room for a short break which lasted approximately 2 minutes. During this time, the experimenter changed the slide tray of the projector. No contacts occurred between the subjects during the break.

When subjects had completed their study of the last slide they were given a questionnaire to complete on their reading interests. This wasn't primarily to collect data but to create a 10 minute time delay between studying the material and completing a criterion test. After exactly 10 minutes, and before any subject could complete it, the questionnaire was collected. The extract below describes the subsequent test procedure.

Immediately after the questionnaire, the criterion recall test was administered, consisting of 12 questions from text slides 1–24 and 22 questions from text slides 25–108. The questions were chosen to have no direct overlap in the content to those of the experimental questions used during the reading. Each question required a one to two word answer. No time limit was set for the test.

The analysis, as indicated in the abstract, indicated that those students who were asked questions by a 'teacher' scored significantly higher on the criterion test than those who responded to the same question in writing – and both groups significantly higher than the control group.

So what is your reaction to the above account? How generalizable are the findings to normal study? What are the features of the report which would support or detract from its generalizability? You can merely think about your reaction, annotate the above account or assemble a series of notes.

Before considering possible reactions to the above account I should say who published it and when. In fact it was written by Ernst Rothkopf and Richard Bloom for the *Journal of Educational Psychology* in 1970 (Rothkopf and Bloom, 1970).

The paper, although over 20 years old, is typical of the experimental studies that have taken place since about 1965 and which are frequently reported in the literature. Indeed, if you were to read recent comprehensive reviews of this type of research (Andre, 1987; Hamaker, 1986; Hamilton, 1985) they would confirm that the experimental tradition in this area of activities in texts attracts many researchers. Assuming you accept that the above example is representative of the experimental studies undertaken in this area, what is your reaction?

I suspect you noted a series of possible features. The actual material used, 16,000 words drawn from four chapters of an earth science textbook, appears reasonable. Certainly, many experiments of this type have been based on extremely brief extracts of material. Unfortunately we do not know if those drawings, photographs, diagrams, etc. that appeared in the original textbook were reproduced, but we could assume they were. However, the context in which the experiment took place can hardly be regarded as normal study conditions! Sitting alone in a portable wooden booth with no opportunity to review previous material, no feedback and no contact with other learners is extremely atypical. Furthermore, a criterion test of one or two word answers suggests low level recall – hardly a major feature of most teaching and learning.

What do other researchers and educationalists say about this sort of research and its generalizability? In reviews of adjunct question research about the time Rothkopf and Bloom published their paper two concerns were emerging. The first was associated with the intellectual content of the materials used in the research; its representativeness of real study material. For example, a researcher reviewing experimental studies of questions in texts remarked:

> Many of the studies reported in this paper employed only factual questions, which is unfortunate if the researchers' interest is in a variety of behaviours that can produce learning (Frase, 1970, p 341).

The other concern was over the generalizability of the experimental findings to other learning contexts. For example, in a review of evidence associated with this type of research, concern was expressed over such generalization to real world situations:

> ... serious application of questioning techniques in the real world of instruction will require knowing why they work and under what conditions (Anderson and Biddle, 1975, p 108).

They observed that the experimental studies were typically conducted upon very small amounts of text, under atypical study conditions, often with short answers/sentence completion requiring a low level response rather than a substantial body of material and wide range in questioning strategies and demands. These criticisms were made against experimental research in general but can obviously be applied to the study reproduced in Activity 2.2.

In subsequent years reviewers of such research have repeatedly raised these concerns. For example, Rickards and Denner, in a substantial review of inserted questions stated:

> Perhaps the issue of greatest importance in adjunct questions research concerns the nature of the adjunct question paradigm ... empirical consideration should be given to letting students review the material to answer the post questions... such a modification should be tested since it represents a more ecologically valid procedure than that which is currently employed. At this present time, one must be wary of making generalisations from studies employing the adjunct question paradigm to question answering in general (Rickards and Denner, 1978, p 342).

Other researchers have recognized and supported this concern. In a review of adjunct question research (Duchastel, 1979) it was noted that, in most studies, students are not permitted to study freely; they cannot review and move forwards and backwards in their texts. Duchastel found that where students are allowed to study freely (for example to go back through the text after encountering post-questions), incidental learning is not enhanced and may even be depressed:

> In these studies then, post questions would seem to have shaped a selective learning strategy whereby attention is focussed primarily on question-related content, sometimes to the detriment of other content (Duchastel, 1979, p 10).

Two researchers had previously acknowledged these remarks in their observation:

> Unfortunately, the bulk of this work [effect of inserted questions on student learning] has been carried out under conditions which make its application to real-life situations of restricted use (Schumacher and Young , 1982, p 1).

They allowed 36 university undergraduate volunteers to study a 3,200 word chapter of a textbook that was relevant to course assessment. Students were allowed to annotate the text, make notes, review the text – to study it in their normal way. Open-ended questions were inserted into the text for the experimental group and both experimental and control groups completed a multiple choice criterion test after study of the chapter was complete. The entire learning episode was recorded on video with ingenious apparatus allowing eye movement to be related to the particular part of a page being studied. Schumacher and Young conclude that inserted questions, of a non-trivial type, do influence students' reading and studying of normal textbook materials. They maintained that findings 'suggest a more active reading interaction with the text than is found in the control subjects' (Schumacher and Young, 1982, p 6). Unfortunately the increase in active interaction noted by Schumacher and Young did not lead to significantly better recall test performance.

Other research studies suggest that when experimental controls are relaxed, or more real life material and conditions allowed, the previously identified findings are undermined. For example, many of the experimental studies allow the student unlimited time to study the text and to consider the questions prior to the criterion test. When the time allowed was restricted, as is often the case in a real study situation, the indirect effect of adjunct questions disappeared. More recent reviews, whilst generally confirming previous trends within experimental studies, have identified available study time as an important constraint upon students' study which directly influences research findings (Carver, 1972; Hamaker, 1986; Wong, 1985). Wong, in a review of 27 studies, observed that:

> ... students' active processing of prose and generation of questions require time. Failure to provide them with sufficient time for those cognitive activities negates the experimenter's intended benefit of self-questioning instruction (Wong, 1985, p 245).

Furthermore, Hamaker, in his rigorous review of over 60 experiments, identified the study time allowed for the experiment as:

> ... a major design feature that may determine not only the size of adjunct-questions effects, but the way in which the pattern of learners' processing activities is changed by adjunct questions (Hamaker, 1986, p 236).

Both reviewers urged researchers to actively consider the effect of available study time upon experimental results. Other reviews of research involving questions in texts have remarked upon the need to conduct studies in real world teaching environments (Andre, 1987; Duchastel, 1983; Hamilton, 1985).

A final concern over the generalizability of experimental findings is whether students in these experiments study in the same way as they do under normal conditions. In a research study involving university undergraduates and realistic study material (Säljö, 1979b) it was reported that students described tackling experimental learning tasks in ways that differed from the way they studied normally even when there was no experimental control over their strategy:

> ... even subjects who report themselves as having once and for all decided never to use a memorising strategy when learning, claim that it is very easy to fall back into this behaviour in an experimental condition. It seemed that there was a strong inclination on the part of students to 'do well' in experimental situations, and this, together with a lack of information about what would be considered a 'good' learning outcome, tended to lead to students adopting a memorising approach (Säljö, 1979b, pp 21–2).

The generalizability of the evidence from many experimental studies involving activities to a self-instructional context is thus in doubt.

Evidence of learning in a natural setting

If there is growing criticism of the experimental research associated with mathemagenic devices, what alternatives have been offered and what evidence is there that these alternatives are not just different but more appropriate? The alternative that I'd like to suggest can be summed up in the above sub-heading – evidence of learning in a natural setting. Several pointers to this alternative style of qualitative research can be found in the above quotations and was expressed succinctly by Entwistle when he remarked:

> ... psychological theories must have 'ecological validity' – that is, the theories must be derived from the settings to which they are applied. Otherwise there can be little confidence placed in the utility of the theory (Entwistle, 1984, p 10).

In recent years there has been a growing emphasis upon the use of qualitative methods to explore and describe student learning; to reveal the interplay of factors which influence their learning. Entwistle writes enthusiastically about this emergent research paradigm and the influence of Parlett and Hamilton's 'Illuminative Evaluation' (Parlett and Hamilton, 1977) and Marton's 'Phenomenography' (Marton, 1981); he explained that:

> The alternative approach seeks an emphatic understanding of what is involved in student learning derived from students' descriptions of

what learning means to them. It involves a shift not just of methodology, but of perspective (Entwistle, 1984, p 13).

Parlett and Hamilton sought to promote a general research strategy which would attempt to describe and explain what was happening in a particular context rather than measure and predict it by preconceived and preselected variables. Their approach was consistent with a 'social anthropology' paradigm in that it was based on observation, enquiry and subsequent explanation – with progressive focusing upon those issues that emerged and which participants believed were important. A central feature of illuminative evaluation is that such an approach involves exploration of the real world with its complex social, psychological and emotional considerations. In their seminal paper Parlett and Hamilton note the dominance of the traditional 'agricultural-botany' paradigm in educational evaluations (characterized by experimental research), where different treatments are measured, factors controlled, correlations derived, cause and effect speculated. They challenge the appropriateness of this paradigm to complex educational contexts and suggest an approach which,

> ... concentrates on the information-gathering rather than the decision-making... . The task is to provide a comprehensive understanding of the complex reality (or realities) surrounding the project: in short, to 'illuminate'. ...the evaluator aims to sharpen discussion, disentangle complexities, isolate the significant from the trivial, and raise the level of sophistication of debate (Parlett and Hamilton, 1972, p 99).

Marton's aim was similar and was to promote a methodology which would describe learning as 'seen through the eyes of the learner', that would explore the world that learners perceive and how they experience learning rather than the one researchers may have already constructed and then use to interpret student performance and comments.

Marton regarded much quantitative research as adopting a first order perspective and described it as 'noumenal'. It was characterized by researchers believing that what was to be measured during the research was already known. The process was merely to quantify it. His alternative was to adopt a second order perspective which he termed 'phenomenal', in which the focus would be on the quality of student learning, what students understand, the context in which learning takes place and their awareness of their own learning. With a colleague, Marton describes this second order perspective:

> Firstly, learning always occurs naturally in a context... instead of describing the context in our own (the researchers') categories... we

try to find the categories in terms of which the students interpret the context... . Secondly, not only does learning always occur in a context but it always has a content as well.... The learner's construction of the learning experience... . Lastly, not only is there a consciousness of the content in the learner but there is a consciousness of his being conscious of it as well... the learner's experience of the act of learning (Marton and Svensson, 1980, pp 473–4).

Marton and his colleague argue that the two perspectives should be regarded as autonomous and complementary but stressed that what is viewed from one perspective cannot be viewed from the other.

At this point I would like to illustrate this shift from an experimental approach to the investigation of activities in texts to a more qualitative one. As in the earlier part of this chapter, I would like to present extracts from published material and through an activity give you the opportunity to consider it.

I've selected a study published by Marton in 1975. There are several reasons for this which are worth noting. If Rothkopf is one of the leading figures in experimental studies associated with activities in texts, then Marton should be regarded as one of the leading figures in qualitative work associated with how people learn. I chose the study in question (Marton, 1975) because its publication date is close to that of Rothkopf which you looked at in Activity 2.1; several of the procedures that Marton adopts can be compared directly with those adopted by Rothkopf and Bloom; and it marks one of the first studies by Marton and his colleagues – studies which have since had a profound effect upon research into how people learn in general and into activities in particular.

I've tried to present the following extracts and my summaries in a similar way to those in Activity 2.1 so that they are more easily compared. I would suggest that you simply read through the following account and form your own judgement as to its worth and the insights it provides.

ACTIVITY 2.3 A published account of some qualitative research

The abstract of the published paper is reproduced below; it will give you an overview of the study.

The failure of a learning-algorithm (which tells the subjects what to do in order to succeed in the learning task) is demonstrated. The experimental group was asked content-neutral questions, intended to induce deep-level processing after each section of the passage to be read. Narrow focusing of attention on the questions themselves resulted in erosion of content, reflected in weak performance on a retention test, and only mentioning (as opposed to commenting on) topics in recall. The deleterious effects persisted over an interval of more than two months.

The material used in the study was the first chapter in an introductory book, *How to Study Politics* written by J. Westerståhl in 1970. Although it was a course text that students would eventually study, none of them had read it before. It consisted of five sections, with separate headings, in which there were 11, 11, 10, 13 and 8 paragraphs respectively. The whole chapter consisted of 4,320 words and included three figures.

The 30 students who took part in the study were contacted by telephone and invited to take part in a learning experiment. A convenient time was agreed upon, participants divided randomly into an experimental group and a control group, and the study carried out individually. The instructions given to all those taking part began as follows:

> We have chosen Chapter 1 of this book. The idea is that you should use this time for thorough reading of this chapter. We have found that it gives the best overall view of the whole subject and the best framework for the rest of the literature. We believe that you will find it useful to read just this chapter thoroughly.

Those allocated to the experimental group then received the following instructions:

> All right. You are now going to read Chapter 1 of this book. When you have finished the chapter you will be asked to relate as much of it as you can remember, and you will be asked questions on the content.
>
> During your reading of the chapter I should like you to stop after each section, that is before each new heading, and I will ask you questions about what sub-sections you think each of these can be divided into and how these are connected with each other and what their relationship is to the aim of the whole section. You should mark off these sub-sections with a pencil. You can do this either while you are reading or when you have finished reading the section. I shall also ask later on both how the various sections are connected with each other and what their relationship is to the aims of the whole chapter. When we have gone through the chapter in this way you may go through it again before you tell me what the whole chapter is about and answer questions on the content.
>
> If you want to, you can begin by glancing through the whole chapter before you start reading. Then you can tell me when you have read the first section. All right, you can start.

The group of students who constituted the control group received the following instructions after the general introduction:

> All right. You are now going to read Chapter 1 of this book. When you have finished the chapter you will be asked to relate as much of it as you can remember, and you will be asked questions on the content. If you want to you can begin by glancing through the whole chapter before you start reading. We want you to read the chapter very thoroughly. Take your time over it and really think over the various points discussed. You can tell me when you have read the chapter. All right, you can start.

Every attempt was made to simulate a natural learning environment. The only person in the room with the student was the person conducting the study, who was involved in 'private reading' when not questioning the students as part of the study. The detailed procedures, presented in the actual paper, indicated that after each section of the chapter was studied the student stopped, as instructed, and the following questions were posed:

What sub-sections do you think there are in this section?
   (say where they start and finish)
Can you summarize the content of each of these sub-sections in one or two sentences?
What is the relationship between the various sub-sections?
What is the relationship between each of the sub-sections and the section as a whole?
Why do they come in this order?
Can you summarize the content of the whole section in one or two sentences?
What is the relationship between this section and the chapter as a whole?

In subsequent sections the student was asked

What is the relationship between this section and the preceding one(s)?
Why do the sections come in this order?

When they had completed their study of the whole chapter the following was said:

You can go through the chapter again if you want to, before you give your summary and answer questions... . All right, now you can tell me what the chapter was about.

A series of 20 questions were then put, individually, to each learner. These questions and corresponding answers constituted the retention test; they were tape recorded and transcribed for subsequent analysis. Two months later the same students were contacted and asked the same questions; they were again tape recorded and transcribed.

The retention test aimed to assess learners' understanding of the chapter – the main ideas and principles; high level intellectual abilities consistent with deep level processing. It consisted of questions to distinguish between pairs of concepts (nine questions); relationships between concepts (four questions); explanation of terms and concepts (three questions); the specification of functions and characteristics (three questions). Only one question required a verbatim answer; apart from this particular question, which could be answered by quoting directly from the text, considerable variation was allowed in all of the others. The actual paper illustrates the marking key that was used. It included actual quotations, descriptions of conceptual relationships, the minimum requirements that would allow an answer to be accepted, even expressions that would and would not be allowed. From this marking key answers were judged either right or wrong. Inter-judge reliability was assessed and shown to be extremely high; 0.98 for the first retention test and 0.96 for the second.

The findings from this study, summarized in the abstract, run counter to what you might have expected. The control group (those who were not primed with an indication of the questions they would be asked in the future) actually spent longer reading the chapter than the experimental group! Of course, if the time spent replying to questions is included, the experimental group did spend considerably more time on the overall task. However, one of the main findings was that the control group performed significantly better on both the first and the repeated retention test, even after a two month delay. Further analysis of the transcripts revealed that the replies from learners in the experimental group were, on average, about half as long as those from the control group. The learners in the experimental group were more likely to 'mention' topics rather than explain them. Indeed, it was this finding that prompted Marton to speak in terms of an erosion of content. Rather than understanding the principles upon which the concepts and ideas were based it appeared that learners merely remembered the term but could not adequately explain it. Further analysis of the transcripts from several learners in the experimental group led Marton to offer an explanation for their unexpected poor performance:

> … a kind of technification of the learning process; the subjects possibly develop a strategy for picking up information that is necessary for answering the (inserted) question which they know they are going to be asked. A fixation on the specific questions, or rather on one of them, may result in their no longer proceeding via the text but rather round it (Marton, 1975, p 12).

So what is your reaction to the above account? How generalizable are the findings to normal study? What are the features of the report which would support or detract from its generalizability? You might want to compare it with the account of the experimental study by Rothkopf and Bloom or against the list of features in Activity 2.1. You can merely think about your reaction, annotate the above account or assemble a series of notes.

I suspect you noted a series of points in the above account. Here are some that I noted and my reaction.

The material selected as the basis of the study, the chapter of a book they would eventually meet in their course, seems eminently appropriate. Its length of over 4,000 words makes it a reasonably substantial piece of text. However, it is the way the study was conducted and the way it tried to create as normal an environment as possible, to simulate the way that people actually learn that makes it differ from the experimental account. I noted the phrases in the quotations where the learner was encouraged to review the material before studying the individual sections as well as after studying them. The decision to conduct the study on an individual basis, with a demanding retention test, further distinguishes it from the experiment.

If you considered the account against the list of features in Activity 2.1 I am sure you judged that it satisfied many of the conditions. It was based on individual interviews, learners were carefully selected and the entire study displayed reflexity (not only could the study be repeated but the actual data in transcripts could be re-analysed). In editing the account I have omitted, or simplified, references to the statistical analyses that were performed; they were essentially techniques to measure the difference in performance on the retention test, the time spent, and so on. In reporting findings that challenge assumptions, and offering explanations, the study contributes to theory building. Indeed, this study marked the start of a whole series of research activities by Marton and his colleagues from which a number of issues have emerged and which have been pursued. Several of these, that seek to describe, explain and understand how students learn are worth brief description.

A study conducted by one of Marton's colleagues (Dahlgren, 1975) aimed to investigate the effect of questions in the experimental manipulation of learning. A group of 38 undergraduates were divided into a control and an experimental group and invited to study two chapters of a relevant textbook. The experimental group received an explanation of the concept of deep level processing, were provided with adjunct questions in the text close to the point where relevant discussion occurred and were encouraged to apply their experience of studying Chapter 1 to Chapter 2. The control group were told to study the Chapters in any way they wished, to make notes, annotate the text, take as long as they wished and to 'concentrate on the text and to read it carefully. Afterwards, they should be prepared to answer a number of questions on the content' (Dahlgren, 1975, p 56).

The study confirmed one of the main findings described in the account of Marton's study. The control group performed better on the criterion test – they produced qualitatively superior answers to criterion questions after studying Chapter 1. The adjunct questions, intended to promote a deep level approach, appeared to depress performance. However, the experimental group performed better on key criterion questions after studying Chapter 2. Dahlgren concluded:

> It is, however, evident that the inserted questions have shaped some kind of technification of the learning process in the experimental subjects, i.e. thinking about the questions stood out as the primary objective (Dahlgren, 1975, p 128).

The performance of this group on the criterion test was equivalent to the highest performing experimental group. One explanation for Dahlgren's findings involved a distinction between two forms of variation in students' approaches to learning tasks; a horizontal dimension and a vertical dimension (Dahlgren, 1975). Dahlgren's horizontal dimension is concerned with which aspects, of a text for example, are attended to. There can be variation in what, or how much, is learnt from reading a text. At the same time there can be variation in a vertical dimension, concerning the level or quality of attention: whether a surface or deep level of approach is adopted. From observing that students in experimental conditions tended to adopt a surface approach, and from reviewing the literature on devices such as in-text questions, Dahlgren concluded:

... the controlling factors derived from the mathemagenic hypothesis probably do not have the ability to create a qualitatively new pattern of learning activities. Rather, the effects on the learning result are to be found in the horizontal variation of the level of attention created by the questions. In other words, these lead to an alternative distribution of learning activities in accordance with the distribution dictated by the demands of the situation as it is expressed in the questions (Dahlgren, 1975, p 41).

More recent research (Fayol, 1987) supports these findings; activities in texts received more reading time and cognitive effort when compared to other parts of the text.

In a further investigation by Marton and his colleagues (Marton and Säljö, 1976) an attempt was made to induce levels of processing by confronting students with different forms of question, designed to promote surface and deep level processing respectively.

This was based on the assumption that knowledge of what is to be tested will influence a student's approach to a learning task. The two groups were given three incomplete chapters from a relevant course textbook. They received no prior instructions about how to study them but were told to be prepared to answer questions on the content. Subsequent interviews with students revealed that those exposed to questions designed to promote surface level processing found them either in line with their expectations or modified their usual strategy to meet the expected requirements from forthcoming questions. For example, students explained:

I thought they were more or less what you might expect to be asked.

... there were only two questions I could answer on the first bit... . All the rest was sort of detailed about figures and I wasn't in the least prepared for that sort of thing (Marton and Säljö, 1976, p 121).

It appeared to be relatively easy to induce surface level processing of the text. However, the group exposed to questions designed to promote deep level processing exhibited less uniform responses. While the questions did succeed in promoting deep level processing for some, other students became 'technified'.

Furthermore, whilst the criterion performance of students identified as taking a surface level approach appeared to be good it was not sustained over a 45-day period. Those taking a deep level approach, however, did show a higher level of retention even on the type of material on which, for immediate testing, superficial processing seems to be efficient (Marton and Säljö, 1976, p 125).

Many of the insights into student learning, reported by Marton and his colleagues, were obtained during interviews and discussions with students, that is, by qualitative research. In a subsequent paper (Marton and Svensson, 1980) the contribution provided by these 'second order perspectives' exploring students' own concerns and questions – that revealed their own perspective rather than the one created by the researcher during experiment or survey – was acknowledged. Other researchers recognized the role of qualitative research in investigations into student learning. Indeed, during a review of OU research into student learning (Nathenson and Henderson, 1980) acknowledgement was given to the work of colleagues who had concluded that:

> ... what appear to be the most important insights on how students use the learning materials are derived from open-ended questions and spontaneous comment, rather than closed-ended feedback questions (Morgan et al, 1980, p 6).

Concluding comments

I trust this chapter and the three activities that have been offered have challenged the dominant position of experimental research and assumptions associated with activities in texts. If it has alerted you to personal preferences for particular styles or traditions of research and to the characteristics of this and alternative styles, I would judge the chapter successful.

Chapter 3

What do writers say about activities?

Writers' assumptions and expectations

In a face-to-face situation a teacher is able to tell, fairly quickly, if the assumptions behind the teaching are valid and to judge whether his or her expectations about a learner's response to a question have been met. The puzzled expressions, plausible but inappropriate responses or acceptable, even novel, replies are the typical indicators. Depending upon the type of response, teachers alter their assumptions and vary their subsequent teaching; it's something teachers do automatically.

In preparing self-instructional material, to be studied in an open or distance learning context, writers have similar assumptions about the way individuals learn, have expectations about how the material will be studied and how learners will respond to the activities in the text. What are your assumptions and expectations about how your current or future self-instructional material will be studied?

A major assumption, shared by many teachers and writers, is that activities are an integral and central part of the teaching. Many regard them as opportunities to realize key objectives with the rest of the teaching material built around them. The corresponding expectation amongst many teachers and writers is that their learners will recognize the central place of activities in their study and by completing them, achieve the objectives. Do you recognize this assumption and corresponding expectation as one that you have?

Indeed, it is extremely common for writers to start their draft by devising the activities that realize the key objectives they are trying to get learners to achieve; it is the spine upon which other materials and media are fixed. In fact it resembles the practice of those involved in programmed learning who started by specifying the instructional objective, designed an activity to realize this objective, provided feedback or a commentary on possible responses and finally devised linking material to the next objective and so on. The follow-up comments provide the springboard into the next activity with additional material supporting the points raised or considered.

However, it would be misleading to suggest that this is the only practice followed. It is not unusual to find writers trying to devise activities for inclusion in the material *after the texts have been written!* According to Derek Rowntree this is like trying to put currants into the cake *after* you have baked it! What about other assumptions and expectations? Activity 3.1 gives you the opportunity to consider them.

(a) What assumptions lie behind the self-instructional materials you will be assembling and the activities you will be devising?

Example:
ASSUMPTION

1. Activities are an integral part of teaching, a way to realize key objectives, with the rest of the material built around them.

2.

3.

(b) What expectations do you have regarding the way in which learners will study your material in general and the activities in particular?

EXPECTATION

Learners will recognize the central place of activities in their study since they provide an opportunity to realize and practise objectives.

So what assumptions, and corresponding expectations, regarding activities and learner use did you identify? I obviously can't know which ones you have listed but I can share with you those listed by other teachers and writers. In surveys of OU authors and discussion with other writers of self-instructional material five major ones have emerged; I've summarized these in Figure 3.1. As I go through them perhaps you would like to consider how they compare with yours and whether you would adopt or reject them.

Assumption 1: Activities are an integral part of the teaching

The most common assumption amongst writers was that the activities were an integral part of their teaching in which they tried to create a tutorial-in-print. Some gave comments consistent with the concept of a reflective action guide while only isolated comments suggested dialogue. This latter assumption is reflected in the comments of many who maintained that:

> My own preference is to see the relationship ideally as one of a fairly complicated dialogue between myself, the reader and others who have written and worked in the area ... to act as a kind of intermediary so to speak, chairing this kind of seminar.

Other writers expressed similar views. Many said they were trying to:

> ... present materials that would approximate to what you would normally get in the best tutorial relationship ... which has help, guidance and expertise.

In achieving this goal, activities were typically drafted and developed alongside other materials. The expectation amongst writers was that students would recognize the central place of activities in the teaching material, enter into a dialogue with the text and achieve the objectives.

Assumption 2: Interest and enthusiasm can be created via activities

During surveys and discussion virtually all writers conveyed an enthusiasm for the subject matter and material presented in their teaching material – even several years after its production! Of course, many expressed some reservations, things they would have done differently next time, but their inherent interest and enthusiasm for the material pervaded their comments. What is more, writers also assumed it was possible to share this interest and enthusiasm by designing activities in which students could experience this for themselves. The writers repeatedly said things like:

> I wanted students to experience some of the personal reaction I had – to share the excitement... to present students with a controversy which they hadn't realized they're in.

Figure 3.1. *Summary of authors' assumptions and expectations*

Assumption behind materials assembled and activities offered	Expectations regarding how materials are studied and response to activities
1. Activities are an integral part of teaching – simulate a tutorial-in-print and are consistent with the reflective action guide	Learners will recognize central place of activities and will interact with them
2. Interest and enthusiasm can be created in activities and conveyed to learners	Learners share author's excitement with activities adding interest and motivation
3. Variety of formats and types of activity available and desirable; contribute to presentation and intellectual demands	Different methods of presentation are part of teaching; learners will appreciate variety provided
4. Structure and order embodied in design of material will guide and control learning	Learners will benefit most if they follow the advice, instructions and sequence suggested
5. Goal to foster learner independence	Learners will think for themselves and have confidence in the views, opinions and arguments they construct

Writers tried to do this in a variety of ways. Activities were designed which provided opportunities to recognize and explore existing perceptions, to explode myths surrounding some topic, to experience the thrill, the passion or the anger associated with a point of view, the elegance of a solution or satisfaction in a resultant quality product. The expectation was that such activities would stimulate interest in the topic during their interaction with the text. In fostering this enthusiasm writers indicated they were trying to personalize the experience for learners; to help them make it their own. Writers expected that learners would share their interest and enthusiasm and that it would motivate them in their studies.

Assumption 3: A variety of formats and types of activity would be presented

The need for variety in one's teaching is something that all teachers are aware of – to avoid the danger of teaching becoming stale through repetitive and predictable exercises. In the same way that variety is built into face-to-face teaching, many writers described how they incorporated activities of differing format and type into their teaching material and how these were designed to contribute variety to both presentation and intellectual demands. Writers typically remarked:

I would try to build variety into the material ... I wouldn't want every activity to be the same ...I had a sense that variety was important. I think that's true of the approach to all teaching.

As in conventional teaching, writers did not have an array of previously prepared formats or types of activity that they intended to engineer into the self-instructional teaching material; they maintained that the very nature of the activity forced one into a different format. Indeed, it was evident that writers were striving for variety throughout all their teaching material with different components making different contributions – retaining and stimulating learner interest and attention. The variety embodied in the activities required a range of intellectual responses. These ranged from recall and comprehension to analysis and evaluation (see Krathwohl et al, 1964). It was assumed that students would both recognize and appreciate this variety.

Assumption 4: Activities contribute to the order and structure of the material

Many writers distinguished between the content of the teaching material they had assembled or were assembling and the form it took. This distinction was expressed clearly by one writer who used the terms 'plot' and 'message'. The message was the

... whole complicated thing that you're...trying to get through to your students with all its complexities and inconsistencies.

The series of points, issues and arguments that are reflected in a collection of readings, quotations, extracts, experiments or exercises, etc. contribute to make up this message. The plot was

... some ordering principle and structure in order to make all this mass of material intelligible.

The activities were regarded as part of this plot in guiding and controlling a learner's study; their design reflected this expectation and individual comments confirmed it. An indication of a writer's attempt to exert control over a person's learning is provided by the comment:

if ... students are really bothered about [completing the teaching material] as it is set up they really ought to go back to that activity.

The provision of a framework in which an optimum route was suggested and flagged by a series of activities was the ordering principle upon which the unit was based and recommended to students.

Assumption 5: Completion of activities would foster learner independence

The fostering of independent learning was a major goal for virtually all writers with activities playing a central role in achieving it. Many writers explained how they were trying to

> Encourage them to ask questions about the material and to see if they can see other interpretations than the ones I'm raising.

In doing this the writers were not attempting to merely transmit a body of knowledge but to actually engage learners in the process of learning; sentiments clearly expressed by one writer:

> … I think it's essential to what I want them to get that they do activities – that they work actively … I'm not actually interested in what position they end up taking on things, I'm very interested in them looking critically at the various positions … I would like that to be what they learn from the activities because that process is very valuable.

In much teaching material a number of competing arguments may be valid and a range of interpretations permissible.   The expectation of many writers was that learners, during a consideration of the argument, viewpoint, interpretation or whatever, would construct their own; learners would think for themselves and have some confidence in the position they adopt.

The five assumptions and expectations summarized in Figure 3.1 provided a framework within which writers were apparently designing activities and integrating them into the text. They reflected a commitment to the concepts of a tutorial-in-print and to a lesser extent the reflective action guide and are likely to be shared by many colleagues designing similar self- instructional material. However, these concepts represent more than the mere studding of traditional, formally-worded texts with questions; it envisages an interaction between learner and teacher. Rowntree (1975) has argued for two-way communication in teaching and learning and suggested that much of our current teaching is one-way and that the aim should be for learners to formulate their own questions and answers. However, there are other influences upon writers, some of which are discussed below.

Influence of other writers and institutional practices

The traditional pattern in conventional education is for teachers to work alone; to plan their lessons independently and to teach them by themselves.

While numerous examples of team teaching are available and its benefits documented, the traditional pattern still predominates. However, in many institutions developing open and distance learning materials this practice is challenged. The division of labour within teams is often the most effective with the contribution of subject matter specialists and other professionals increasingly recognized. In this context the OU course team model has achieved international prominence, (Perry, 1976) but it is not the only one possible (Riley, 1983). Others have been used successfully in a variety of institutions (see Crick, 1980, Stringer, 1980) and are worth examining.

Three different methods of materials production, termed 'personalised training', 'workshop generated' and 'text transformation' were described in a recent article (Lockwood, 1992). Personalized training is designed to equip writers with those skills and techniques they need to deploy when planning and producing self-instructional material *at the moment in time when they need them*. Personalized training was adopted within the team that devised the National Association of Clinical Tutors training package described earlier.

When appropriate teaching material is not available, or doubt is expressed as to its existence, *it can be readily generated in a workshop context by subject matter specialists*. A group of doctors, nurses, practice managers, educationalists and medical writers over a single weekend generated the material that eventually became the resource package *Coronary Heart Disease Prevention Programmes* (The Medicine Group, 1991). The package contained guidelines, discussion points, resources and activities. An example of an activity, in the form of a pre-test 'What do you know about a successful lipid-lowering diet?' is given in Example 3.1.

When materials are already in existence, but are considered to be inadequate for their intended purpose, *they can be transformed into high quality distance teaching materials* by the process of text transformation. The computer-based exercises, developed by Cardiff University College, that were transformed into the computer-assisted learning materials called POPTRAN (Henderson et al, 1988) are typical of this process; Example 3.2 is an activity from this material. Note the use of icons, facsimile of a computer screen and student stopper.

Whether the planning, production and presentation of your self-instructional material is undertaken alone, or involves a group of colleagues, it is likely that it will be influenced by a variety of institutional pressures and practices; but what might these be? Let's take the institutional pressures first, before we go on to consider the actual practices that may have evolved amongst you and your colleagues regarding the design of activities in texts.

I'm aware that many institutions are working under difficult financial

Example 3.1 *Lipid-lowering diet* (The Medicine Group, 1991)

What do you know about a successful lipid-lowering diet?
Answer the questions by ticking the appropriate boxes.

1. When giving dietary advice for lowering blood cholesterol levels, which is the most important factor to consider?

Total fat intake ☐

Cholesterol intake ☐

2. Consumption of all types of dietary fibre should be encouraged, though one type has a cholesterol-lowering effect. Which one is it?

Soluble fibre in beans, lentils and oats ☐

Insoluble fibre like cellulose and lignin found in cereals ☐

3. Which of the following foods contain more than 10% fat?

Dairy ice cream ☐   Garibaldi biscuit ☐

Roast chicken meat only ☐   TUC biscuit ☐

Cooked ham ☐   Stilton cheese ☐

Low-fat spread ☐   Edam cheese ☐

Semi-skimmed milk ☐   Whole milk ☐

Rich Tea biscuit ☐

4. Which of the following fats have the same calorific value as butter?

Hard margarine ☐

Polyunsaturated margarine (e.g. Flora) ☐

Low-fat spread ☐

Dairy-fat spread (e.g. Krona, Clover) ☐

5. Are monounsaturated fats 'goodies' or 'baddies' in the fight to reduce cholesterol levels?

Goodies ☐

Baddies ☐

6. For a person on a diet low in fat to reduce blood lipids, what would be an acceptable egg intake?

6 eggs/week ☐

3 eggs/week ☐

1 egg/week ☐

7. What percentage of the total daily calorie intake should be provided by fat?

10% ☐   20% ☐   30% ☐   40% ☐   50% ☐

What is the current national average intake?

Compiled by Liz Eeley, Senior 1 Dietitian, John Radcliffe Hospital, Oxford

Answers on reverse

Example 3.2 *Population projections* (Cardiff University College, 1986)

1.9   The POPTRAN program provides the opportunity for you to select from four graphic displays of this data.

     • Press 1 to obtain Display 2 for the Sudan.

Display 2   Population Change for the Sudan 1985-2085

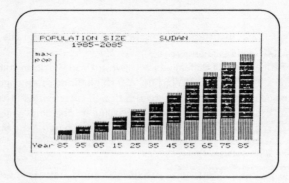

1.10   Each of the vertical columns represents the total population of the country in that particular year. The column is made up of three shaded portions which represent, from the base of the column upwards, the Age Cohorts 0-14, 15-65 and 65-80+. A cross-check with the year 1985 (first column in Display 2 and first row in Display 1) indicates that there were:

         9.46 million (44.6%) under 15 years;
         0.63 million (2.9%) over 65 years; and therefore
         11.12 million (52.5%) between these ages.

1.11   **?**   What would be the size of these Age Cohorts (in millions and percentage terms) in the year 2085?

❂ ❂

1.12   The population of the Age Cohorts 0-14 would have grown to 43.20 million (24.7%). Those aged over 65 would have increased to 14.45 million (8.3%). There would be 117.34 million (67%) between these ages.

     At the end of the projection there would be about five times as many under 15, and about 20 times as many over 65, than at the start. There would also be a larger proportion in the working population: about 33% of the population would be over-65s and under-15s at the end of the projection period, as opposed to 47% at the beginning.

constraints, with staff being asked to undertake an increasing variety of roles, and additional developments such as staff appraisal, new curricula, etc. but I'd like you to put these pressures on one side and think in terms of how your colleagues interact as a group; what are the social pressures and relationships that exist which shape the operation of the group? This certainly isn't an easy task and if you think you are immune from such influences you may have to think again, as I hope Activity 3.2 will illustrate.

ACTIVITY 3.2 Institutional pressures and influence on the team

I'd like you to consider the group of colleagues with whom you work, or may have worked in the past, and how they operate as a group. What do you think binds them together, what is divisive and how might this manifest itself in relation to the design of activities in texts?

Recognizing these pressures is a useful starting point in deciding which to foster for your mutual good and which may be adversely affecting your teaching. You may want to jot down your ideas.

Let me describe a possible scenario and suggest how the social and group pressures operate. I will assume that the production of self-instructional material is to be undertaken as a collaborative effort extending over several months. I will also assume that the project involves both senior and junior colleagues, some of whom have little experience of writing self-instructional material, others who have produced several open learning packages. In such a situation it is likely that success will be dependent upon establishing and maintaining a close or at least harmonious working relationship as the more experienced individuals share their experience with others. It is quite common in such situations for an experienced member of the institution to prepare various briefing documents to explain and illustrate the course production process and role of component parts. However, the most powerful influence on the attitude and behaviour of group members is likely to occur informally in conversation with other writers whilst working within the group and with colleagues within the institution. This environment is central to their socialization into course production in general and into the accepted practices of the institution. It is this social pressure that binds the team together.

Discussions with writers have repeatedly identified the influence of colleagues who have had a major impact on the way they design activities; such writers have remarked:

> This was the first [self-instructional material] I constructed ... I remember listening very intently to what other people were saying.

> … because of conversations I'd had with members of the team I had fairly strong views about the use of activities within [my teaching] and tried to engage people actively in the text.

The power of these socializing factors is considerable, even for those who initially challenge institutional guidelines. For example, a staff member new to the production of self-instructional material in general and activities in particular contrasted the prescribed role of activities with practices elsewhere and in other printed materials. He argued that:

> … most print you learn from doesn't have activities… we are talking about a particular academic subculture that lives [here], and subcontracted acolytes… required to accept the tribal law.

However, even though he made this observation he accepted the 'tribal law' and his subsequent material followed the institutional pattern of trying to create a tutorial-in-print or offered activities consistent with a reflective action guide.

The team and other colleagues thus exert a strong influence upon writers in communicating institutional practice in general and that which would be appropriate to a particular teaching package. The reason is that it is inevitable that the assumptions and expectations embodied in you and your colleagues will, over time, become the *accepted ways of doing things* that influence others. It is the insidious nature of these pressures and practices that results in their gaining widespread acceptance.

However, it would be misleading to suggest that under the pressure of producing teaching materials, conflicts do not emerge which can be divisive. Indeed, anyone who has been involved with a group of colleagues in the production of teaching materials, unless they have been particularly fortunate, will have observed and experienced tensions,

> … between individuals, team and organisation over control of schedules, between high expectations for courses and the limited resources or between academic quality and teaching effectiveness (Nicodemus, 1992, p4).

Nicodemus has worked with many individuals and teams in helping them identify, articulate and resolve the divisive tensions that can be associated with the organization and dynamics of team work. In the context of learning materials production he has identified a series of dimensions that can be at the heart of interpersonal conflict, although he admits that there is no '…orderly unfolding of anxieties directly related to the time and space of the course process.' (Nicodemus, 1992, p9).

One of the dimensions that Nicodemus identifies is termed 'academic/

administration'. Within this dimension he illustrated the tensions that arose in an OU team in relation to the production schedule when a fellow academic (writer), who also had the role of team leader, was increasingly perceived by his colleagues as favouring the position and concerns of the 'administration' rather than that of the 'academic'; some 'academics' supported the position taken by the 'administration', others supported their colleague who was behind schedule. Other dimensions around which tensions have repeatedly emerged have been described as teaching/research – between assembling teaching material and representing the research that underpins it; presentation/learner support – between the self-instructional nature of the material and the forms of support that should be available; media/control – between the technical processes involved in media creation and academic control over the resultant product; design/production – between the layout and design techniques available and the costs of using them.

If you accept the socializing influence of the group we can move on to a consideration of the institutional practices that develop from them. Of course, the very nature of institutional practices, where the individuals are closely involved in them, makes them difficult to identify – because they are so commonplace and accepted. In this context the difference between writers' stated assumptions with regard to activities and what they actually do, as illustrated in their finished material, resembles the distinction between 'espoused theories' and 'theories-in-use' (Argyris and Schön, 1974). It is the difference between what you and your colleagues say you do and what you actually do.

For example, the briefing documents provided to new OU authors state the espoused theories (Open University, 1984). Subsequent course team discussion at a course planning stage and when commenting on draft materials reinforce it (Riley, 1983). The persuasiveness of these espoused theories is evident in any description or illustration of OU teaching material; activities in texts have become a characteristic. It is also reflected in the comments of individual authors as illustrated above.

However, Argyris and Schön observed that individuals may be unaware of the discrepancy between espoused theories and theories-in-use:

> We value the consistency of our theories-in-use and our behavioural worlds. Hence, theories-in-use tend to be self maintaining. We tend to adopt strategies to avoid perceiving that data do not fit, that behavioural reality is progressively diverging from one's theory of it, that one's theory is not tested out ... One goes on speaking in the language of one theory, acting in the language of another and maintaining the illusion of congruence through systematic self-deception.' (Argyris and Schön, 1974, pp 32–3).

Could this observation be applied to you and your colleagues? Activity 3.3 and the associated discussion provide an opportunity for you to consider the extent to which you do actually implement your espoused theories or have begun to apply the theories-in-use that have emerged through institutional practice. However, this is by no means an easy task. Argyris and Schön maintain that one's recognition of inconsistencies between espoused theories and theories-in-use requires self-awareness and honesty to articulate. It can be a painful and sobering exercise.

However, thinking in terms of the design of activities within your self-instructional material, what are the *accepted ways of doing things* that you can identify that may influence your design of activities? Some of these may be based on sound theory and research and contribute to learning; others may have simply evolved and have effects that are counterproductive. Activity 3.3 will help you start the process of looking at your existing practices and questioning them.

ACTIVITY 3.3 Institutional practices

Can you identify those design practices that are accepted by members of your group or institution which are likely to influence your design of activities? In an attempt to help you start this process I've listed several areas in which such factors may operate. By considering each one in turn you will be able to assess their likely or actual influence, as well as being able to identify others that may be present.

  a.   What is the optimum number of activities to provide in a text?

  b.   Where are the activities and follow-up comments positioned?

  c.   How are activities identified or flagged in the text?

  d.   What provision is made for a response?

  e.   What are the intellectual levels at which activities are pitched?

  f.   What types of response are required to complete activities?

  g.   How much time is allocated for the completion of activities?

---

a. What is the optimum number of activities to provide in a text?

What is the typical practice that you and your colleagues follow and is it consistent? Do you adopt a policy of posing an activity every few pages of text or after so many minutes of study; a policy similar to that often espoused by teachers who maintain that 15 to 20 minutes is the longest most learners can concentrate before they need a different stimulus? Or do you regard the number of activities as one that is dictated by the material under study; that if the activities are to realize key objectives then the number and nature of the objectives will determine the number of activities?

Another look at examples of the material you and your colleagues have produced may give an indication of the practice(s) you adopt. Of course, within such practices there are two possible extremes, as well as numerous variations. At one extreme, writers have maintained that in striving to assemble an interactive text the entire material has become a series of activities; at the other, activities have been completely omitted. An example of these extreme practices was noted by researchers at the OU when exploring students' reactions to activities during a postal survey of a social science and technology course (Duchastel and Whitehead, 1980). These authors reported that in the same course, in adjacent course units, several different approaches to the inclusion of activities and the terminology used were apparent. These ranged from integrating over 20 activities (12 exercises and 10 SAQs) in a text of about 40 pages of teaching material, through a similar amount of teaching material with about half this number of activities, to a teaching text with no activities in it whatsoever. They also noted that in some units SAQs were related directly to an objective and provided an opportunity to review the teaching material; exercises were interspaced in the text and were designed to encourage interaction with the text. In other units SAQs were not related to objectives and did not review the material – this was performed by the exercises! The researchers remarked:

> It is always important to bear in mind that in-text questions... can serve different purposes and often come under a variety of labels, which are not always consistent even within a given course [as in this particular case] (Duchastel and Whitehead, 1980, p 44).

In their discussion of the survey findings, Duchastel and Whitehead comment on the confusing and inconsistent terminology used in the same course, but despite this they also report the extremely high proportions of students completing the activities. They also state that for the unit that did not contain any activities, nearly 60 per cent of students said their absence hindered their study, with none saying it helped!

b. Where are the activities and follow-up comments positioned?

If you were to ask a group of classroom teachers when they posed questions in their lessons, or when the main activity or activities in the lessons take place, the immediate response, I suspect, would be ' ... all the time', or '... the entire lesson is built upon or around them'. Similarly, if you asked the same group when they give feedback on learners' answers to questions, or comment upon their learners' performance on activities, I suspect they would say they give constant feedback or as soon after the task has been completed as possible. Let me pose the same questions to you. Where do you position activities and corresponding follow-up comments in your self-instructional teaching material? If you spent a few minutes of your time skimming through some examples of your material, and that of your colleagues, you might identify certain patterns or trends in the positioning of these activities and be able to consider the implications of doing so.

Whilst there are numerous possibilities, three formats are the most common:

i.   Throughout the text – at the point when the questions are posed with immediate follow-up comment.
ii. In a separate activity booklet – to which the learner is referred for both the task(s) and feedback provided.
iii. Grouped at the beginning or end of sections – as pre- or post-tests, with answers grouped in a series of appendices.

i. Throughout the text – at the point when the questions are posed with immediate follow-up comment.

Posing questions in the text, as they arise, is consistent with the concept of a tutorial-in-print mentioned previously and is often the most natural and engaging method to adopt. However, while many writers are able to integrate activities into their teaching texts they often seem reluctant to provide unrestricted access to the accompanying follow-up comments.

A practice adopted in some early self-instructional material was to provide a separate 'masking card' that the learner could position over the page to prevent accidental sight of the follow-up comments. Whilst this practice is now seldom used it is certainly not unusual for a learner, after completing an activity, to be directed to the back of the document for the answer or discussion of possible answers. In extreme cases such feedback has been printed upside down in an attempt to 'prevent cheating'! The evidence from interviews with students indicates that such ploys are counterproductive. Positioning follow-up comments at the back of texts is typically felt to be unnecessary whilst printing them upside down irritates. What is more, these practices certainly do not prevent those who are determined to ignore the question and turn immediately to the answer. Certainly, the principle of immediate reinforcement should apply to follow-up comment in just the same way as it does to other teaching practices. In the majority of cases a discussion of the tasks posed in the activity can commence immediately after the activity; its immediacy is valued by learners. In those cases where it is felt that a brief answer positioned directly below the activity could be be seen inadvertently – like a number, formula, symbol, simple name or phrase – it may be worth arranging the page so that the learner has to turn to the following page to read it. (See Duchastel and Whitehead [1980] for an account of how students explained how they inadvertently saw answers.)

The aim should be to encourage learners to engage with the material and to do all possible to facilitate smooth progress in the material – a practice not aided by repeatedly having to turn to other places in the text.

ii. *In a separate activity booklet – to which the learner is referred for both the task(s) and the feedback provided.*

If posing questions in the text as they arise is the most natural and engaging method to adopt why would anyone hive them off into a separate activity booklet? One possible reason is financial. Generating the bulk of the self-instructional material and integrating activities can be a time-consuming exercise and result in expensive print costs. Producing *wrap around texts* or entering into collaborative publishing arrangements can reduce both production time and print costs considerably. In a *wrap around text* procedure one or more existing texts are identified and constitute the bulk of the teaching. They may be single-authored texts, anthologies or commissioned articles. Supplementary material, often in the form of a study guide, is wrapped around these texts. This material contains any directions, guidelines, activities and comments that the writer believes are necessary to obtain maximum benefit from the existing texts. In such a system the institution may save considerable time by not having to write material that is already available – but then has to decide whether to provide the existing texts as part of the course material or to pass this cost on to the learner.

In recent years an increasing number of courses have been designed in collaboration with commercial publishing companies. The advantage to the teaching or training organization is that the considerable cost of course production is shared with the publisher. The publisher acquires several new titles, a guaranteed market over a period of years and potential sales beyond. However, in such arrangements there is often pressure to separate the 'academic' or 'training' content from the teaching material, so that the centrally published material is available to the widest possible audience and not restricted to one. In such arrangements a separate study guide or activity booklet is a common solution. The learners can retain their study guide and the institution decides whether to let them have the associated texts or to use them again with future students.

iii. *Grouped at the beginning or end of sections – as pre- or post-tests, with answers grouped in a series of appendices.*

When commencing a new topic or meeting a group of learners for the first time there are a number of ways in which you can determine the level at which to pitch the teaching. You can rely upon your previous experience of teaching this material, your knowledge of this particular group of students, or you can assemble a simple diagnostic test. However, in an open or distance learning context you may never have met your learners, taught the material before and have no opportunity for administering diagnostic tests – or do you?

It is not unusual for those engaged in open or distance learning to bring with them to the material a variety of interests, experiences and abilities; they invariably represent a heterogeneous group. If this is the case, assembling a single set of materials, through which all learners are led, may not be the most appropriate. Instead, it may be worth devising a series of activities, or pre-tests, by which learners can judge whether they need the corresponding material or not; it is a practice that is widely used to good effect. For example, when the OU was assembling its preparatory material to precede the mathematics foundation course (Open University, 1985b) the learners were first directed to a series of activities, a diagnostic quiz, that acted as pre-tests. Depending upon one's performance on these activities, you were advised to either study the material in a corresponding section or not. At one extreme the evaluation revealed that some students completed all the pre-tests in about 20 minutes and were informed that they already had all the mathematics skills and techniques they would need to start the foundation course. At the other extreme were students who discovered that their mathematical competence was such that they needed to study all the corresponding sections, and took 180 hours to do so (Lockwood, 1989). Example 3.3 illustrates an extract from a recent version of the diagnostic quiz that focused upon algebra – the manipulation of symbols. Is there a role for activities of this type in your teaching material? If so it may be appropriate to group them together in a separate section or booklet together with the follow-up material.

c. How are activities identified or flagged in the text?

If you have had the opportunity to look through examples of self-instructional materials, such as those produced by the Open University, the Open College and the National Extension College in the UK and numerous national providers overseas, I suspect you can identify a whole variety of ways in which activities could be identified in the text. A few illustrations are provided in Examples 1.1 to 1.12 in Chapter 1.

A common device to alert the reader of self-instructional text to an imminent activity is the 'student stopper'. This often takes the form of a narrow frieze across the page (as in Example I.2), a row of keyboard characters (as in Example 1.8), or a bold line similar to that illustrated in

Example 3.3 *Pre-test of algebraic skills* (Open University, 1990)

2 Algebra : Manipulating Symbols

2.1 Translating words into mathematical expressions is a very important skill.

(i)   Can you express the following sequence of instructions as an algebraic expression, using x to stand for the unknown number?
"Think of a number. Square it. Add four and multiply by -8. Add twice the number you first thought of. Divide by 2."

(ii) (a)   Now simplify the expression by removing the brackets. What is the coefficient of x^2?

(b)   What is the value of this expression when $x = 2$? Check your answer by carrying out the instructions one by one.

2.2 You will need to be able to do various kinds of algebraic manipulation when handling equations and formulae. Try these, simplifying your answers as much as possible.

(i)   (a)   Write down an algebraic expression for the perimeter of this rectangle.

(b)   Write down an algebraic expression for the area of the rectangle.

(ii) Evaluate the area when $a = 20$ metres and $b = 2$ metres.

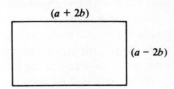

2.3 Here is a question designed to test whether you can juggle symbols past an equality sign. The formula below is called the lens formula and is used in physics. It is normally quoted in the form given below but it is sometimes useful to have it in other forms.

$$\frac{1}{f} = \frac{1}{u} + \frac{1}{v}$$

(i)   Rearrange this expression so that it has the form

$u = \ldots.$

(ii) Suppose that v is equal to u.

(a)   Rearrange the resulting expression in the form

$f = \ldots.$

(b)   Here's a bit more jargon. Can you now say whether f is directly proportional or inversely proportional to u?

Example 3.1. They are a carry-over from the programme learning days when a teaching text was divided into a series of small segments or frames and the intention was to typographically flag the key question that would dictate future progress within the programme. More recently icons and typographical symbols have been incorporated into the text to assist with this basic task. The variety in these icons is enormous, they range from question marks to traffic lights, quill pens and pencils to Rodin's 'The Thinker', facsimiles of 'men at work' signs to words and phrases in the text saying, 'self assessment question (SAQ)', 'In-text questions (ITQ)', activity or exercise – several of these are illustrated in the above examples. Activities have been typographically flagged by indenting the text, putting it in a box, using a different type face or colour, be this coloured type, use of half tones or coloured paper.

Although the growth in the use of word processing and desk top publishing packages has dramatically increased the options available to writers to identify and flag the activities in their texts, a question, accompanied by a question mark, remains the simplest way of posing a question. All of these features contribute to establishing the 'house style' that is synonymous with institutional practice. All this is based on the assumption that every activity is flagged in the text; but what if they are not flagged, what if they are buried or submerged in the text like an iceberg – only the very tip is exposed?

It is not unusual for writers to strive towards producing an interactive teaching text and to devise a large number of worthwhile activities and for these to be incorporated into the teaching material. The problem arises when they have to flag the numerous activities, and allocate time and space to them, only to find they are way over the page or study time allocation for that material. This problem is a common one and was apparent during discussions with writers. Their teaching material did contain numerous questions but they were only elevated to the level of an activity on a small number of occasions. Many remain buried in the text; a feature recognized by one writer when considering the following extract from his teaching text:

2.5 How do your own experiences as a pupil or as a parent compare? Were you a 'counter-cultural' or 'official' chooser, or perhaps you recall different categories? Have you children who have sought advice from you? If so, how did you advise them, and why? What difficulties did you experience? How did you relate to the school and teachers concerned? If you are not a parent, you might imagine these circumstances. If you are a teacher, how do you view this interpretation of these processes? Also, look back over your notes on the relationships between parents and professionals in Unit 6 (Open University, 1981, p 38).

He remarked

> ... this is a bit of an activity I suppose although it's not actually listed as one... a number of questions again, it's not listed as an activity but it really is one built into the text.

An implication of elevating some of the more obvious questions and tasks to an activity, assuming the material under consideration has been allocated a specific amount of time in the overall programme of study, is that the amount of study time available for other course materials is reduced. This can create a major difficulty facing writers who often feel the need for pages of text and time in which to assemble their teaching material. Whereas some writers systematically underestimated the amount of time allocated to activities (see below), others buried them in the text and either assumed that not all of them would be completed by students or merely left it for the learner to decide which to attempt. The following remark is typical: 'I wouldn't expect them to do every bit of it to the same degree, it would take them weeks to do it'. (Unfortunately, very few teaching texts actually tell learners that the activities are a resource and are optional – the implication is that all the components are worthwhile and ought to be studied.)

Does this strike a chord with you? Have you and your colleagues created and operated institutional practices where you simply bury activities in the text to save you time, and solve one of your problems, but leaving your learners with the dilemma whether to respond to the questions or not? Of course, a momentary response to those buried in the text would not add significantly to the workload, but would diminish the learning experience you envisaged. Becoming engaged with the activity could well improve the learning experience of your students but at a cost in terms of the study time consumed – maybe one not recognized by the institution.

d. What provision is made for a response?

Do you and your colleagues make provision for the response you expect learners to make and is this consistent? Do you leave a space in the text, design a grid, framework or matrix within which learners can enter their response? Do you expect them to scribble in the margin or write their answers in a separate file? In any discussion of the above questions issues of cost and pedagogy typically emerge.

Any organization assembling self-instructional material will obviously need to consider all the attendant costs, including print costs. During such considerations it is not unusual for observers (accountants) to point out that a number of printed pages could be saved if the space devoted to activities was omitted and learners asked to respond to the activity on a separate piece of paper or in the margin. Such observers have obviously failed to appreciate that the blank space in teaching texts is often as important as the space taken up by the print!

Such practices would obviously save money – but how much and at what cost? In the context of materials production, the actual cost of print is extremely small, even if commercial printers are employed. If you doubt this, why not contact a commercial printer and investigate how much it would cost to run off a hundred copies or so of a teaching text if you were to provide camera ready copy. The major cost is in terms of people: writers, editors, designers and the like. Furthermore, the cost of such a decision, in educational terms, could be considerable. There is relatively little evidence concerning the space provided for an response to an activity, but that described below is persuasive.

Several years ago, during the developmental testing of the OU arts foundation course, student responses to 165 activities were recorded (Henderson, 1977). The activities were distinguished in terms of whether they posed closed-ended or open-ended questions. (Closed-ended questions were those requiring a tick or a cross, a number or letter or a simple word or phrase as an answer. Open-ended questions were those requiring the student to assemble several sentences into an argument, case or response.) After analysing student replies Henderson drew several conclusions which are extremely relevant to the question of whether space should be provided for an answer and the form it should take. He noted that closed-ended questions, when a framework or grid was provided, were answered by extremely large proportions of students; typically over 90 per cent. For open-ended questions, when no space was provided, student responses fell dramatically to less than 40 per cent. However, when space was provided for open-ended questions the typical proportion of students responding to them rose to nearly 90 per cent. His simple conclusion was:

1. *Closed-ended ITQs motivate high proportions of students to attempt them.*
2. *Students are more likely to respond to an open-ended ITQ if an appropriate space is provided in the text for them to write their answers* (Henderson, 1977, p 5).

It is not only more convenient to write an answer in a space provided in the text but, as Henderson remarked, if you decide that a written response is desirable the size of the space will give an indication of the length of answer expected. An indication of the study time that would be typically expected, or guidance to answer in two or three sentences or 50 words may give just the advice that is needed.

These general conclusions were confirmed recently (Lockwood, 1990) when OU students studying a course within the faculty of educational studies described how they reacted to the provision of a grid, framework or space for an answer. Even those learners who maintain they seldom attempt activities report themselves being inextricably drawn into doing it:

> There was a little grid and you had to add things . . . I just remember writing things in boxes and I was quite surprised with myself because I've never done that before.

Example 3.4 shows activities which did and which did not provide a framework for a response.

This is not the place to enter into a discussion of font sizes, typographical grids and the layout and design of textual material. For those interested there are some excellent sources of information and advice (Hartley, 1985; Misanchuk, 1992). Sufficient to say that the informed layout and design of textual materials can enhance their teaching effectiveness, provide advance organizers and enable the learner to gain and maintain access to the text.

e. What are the intellectual levels at which activities are pitched?

The nature of your subject matter will dictate the extent to which intellectual, emotional and practical tasks are undertaken within your self-instructional material, but your design of activities will determine the level at which they are pitched. At what cognitive, affective and psychomotor levels do you and your colleagues typically pitch your activities? Does your material contain activities pitched at a range of levels, do they progress through a series of levels or do they concentrate on one particular level? A worthwhile exercise would be to select a piece of self-instructional material that you have written, or with which you are familiar, and without detailed inspection estimate the proportion of activities at each of the main levels. You can then consider each of the activities in the material and determine exactly the proportion of activities at each level and whether this is appropriate for the learners in question and this stage in their study.

Frameworks have been devised by which it is possible to categorize intellectual or cognitive activities (Bloom et al, 1956), emotional or affective activities (Krathwohl et al, 1964) and practical or psychomotor (Harrow, 1972). They may help you to categorize the activities within the material you are considering.

So what was the outcome of your impromptu check on the material? Were your original estimates substantiated by a systematic categorization? What implications may this have for your learners? Several researchers have noted the importance of pitching activities at an appropriate level and their treatment by learners if the level is inappropriate. For example, during the investigation of the activities within the OU arts foundation course (Henderson, 1977) it was concluded that those activities that were pitched at a low level, that were perceived as trivial, were invariably ignored. Learners repeatedly mentioned that they treated activities with the respect (or contempt) that their intrinsic merits deserved. (Their intrinsic merit was typically related to their relation to the course objectives.) However, the effect of posing trivial, low level activities also had major implications for future study. Henderson (1977, p 4) reported that, '. . . a series of [activities] which are perceived as trivial is likely to discourage students from attempting further [activities]'.

Another investigation of an OU materials science course (Nathenson, 1978) confirmed the above findings. It also revealed that when students were not adequately prepared for an activity they simply skipped it.

Indeed, this tendency for learners to react adversely to activities, and for this reaction to be applied to all subsequent activities, was noted in more recent research (Lockwood, 1990). A typical student remark was:

> Once I have geared myself up to not bothering too much about the activities, which I must admit I haven't bothered much with, I just do the reading.

There are thus obvious dangers of pitching activities at inappropriate levels.

Do you realize what I've just done – besides talking about the levels at which activities are pitched? I've 'buried' an activity in the text and left you with the decision whether to respond to the questions I posed or not! I hope I made it sufficiently tantalizing so that you actually thought about finding the books I quoted, seeing how they categorize cognitive, affective and psychomotor activities and assigning your own activities within these frameworks. Of course, if I had given you the frameworks, perhaps with a 'thumb-nail' sketch of each category in the system and flagging it in the text as an activity, you may have been more inclined to do it.

At the start of section f. below I have illustrated just how easy it is to 'bury' an activity in the text; this time I've been a bit more subtle.

f. What types of response are required to complete activities?

If you are trying to simulate a tutorial in print, a reflective action guide or

Example 3.4 *Absence or provision of a grid or framework for a response* (Open University, 1981, pp 19 and 26)

3.13   Whether the avoidance of confrontation is seen as signalling order or disorder, the maintenance of discipline by the teacher, or his failure to maintain it, therefore depends on various considerations. One possibility is that such avoidance may be used for different reasons on different occasions. Another is that it might also be subject to different interpretations depending, to some extent, on who is doing the interpreting. Most people like to place themselves in a favourable light and few care to admit defeat, even to themselves. This needs to be borne in mind when assessing the accounts provided by teachers and pupils of classroom proceedings.

Activity 5
Allow about 15 minutes

At this point you should reread Reading 2.7 in Reader 2, this time paying particularly close attention to the section on confrontation avoidance and to the transcript. Compare your interpretation of the transcript with the author's. Is his conclusion that the teachers are avoiding confrontation with Charlie justified? If so, how effective is the strategy? Does your evaluation of its effectiveness vary depending on whether you are employing short-term or long-term criteria? As in the case of showing up, mentioned earlier, is it possible to specify the conditions in which avoiding confrontation does or would work? If so, what are these conditions? On the basis of transcript and 'background' evidence, can the teachers' use of avoiding confrontation be construed as the imposition of their own definition of the situation, as their conforming to Charlie's definition of the situation, or as their redefining the situation in terms of the options that Charlie and the other pupils make available?

3.14   There is not space here to provide my own answers to each question, but my general view is that confrontation avoidance is part of a limited repertoire forced upon teachers by the lack of available alternatives (such as examinations or threats), and that it must be used sparingly in relation to other strategies in order to have any effect. Its benefits for the teacher are probably short term (it enables her to sidestep unpleasant classroom incidents), and if overemployed, pupils may well attempt to provoke further confrontation and increase their misbehaviour in the process. Discretion in the use of this strategy, like most others, seems to be essential.

4.16   At this point it is legitimate to ask what might be meant by the term 'invisible pedagogy' and to what extent empirical research in classrooms confirms its existence in the form suggested by Bernstein.

Activity 7
Allow about ten minutes

In many ways, the concept of an *invisible pedagogy* seems to bear some similarities to the concept of the *hidden curriculum* discussed in Unit 9. You should jot down a one-sentence definition of the hidden curriculum to remind you of the relevant arguments in Unit 9. If you are unable to write such a definition, go back to Unit 9 to refresh your memory.

One of the most teasing questions that can be asked about the hidden curriculum is 'from whom is it hidden?' In Unit 9, the hidden curriculum was seen to be hidden from four possible groups (depending on the definition of 'hidden curriculum' that was being used). Which groups are these?

1 _____   3 _____

2 _____   4 _____

The answers are in the appendix. To which of these groups is the invisible pedagogy invisible?

4.17   Ronald King (1979) has attempted to answer this very tricky question by matching the results of his detailed investigation of infant school classrooms against Bernstein's theory of the invisible pedagogy. Here are three extracts from his analysis;

a dialogue then the type of response you ask for to an activity is limited only by your imagination – and perhaps your own preference. What types of response do you and your colleagues typically call for in the activities you pose? If you have been referring to an example of self-instructional material in response to some of the above questions then it may be easy for you to skim this material again and determine the pattern of responses you have asked for. Are these mainly written or do they involve a variety of replies?

Written replies tend to be the most common, so that the learner has a permanent record to refer to at some future time and to compare with your follow-up comment. These written replies can obviously vary from a single word or phrase to a more substantial piece of material. Of course, a relatively simple form of response isn't to be confused with a simple, or trivial question. The question itself could be quite demanding with several plausible but inappropriate answers. Anyone who has attempted some of the high level multiple choice questions will confirm that even with a list of alternatives to choose from the task of deciding upon an answer can be challenging; assembling a succinct written reply equally so.

Questions, of the type deployed in a dialogue, can be extremely provocative and can encourage a learner to pause for a moment to consider the point made before continuing to read the text. Indeed, just like in a conventional teaching situation, where you may ask your learners to think about an answer to a question before you elaborate, you can design similar questions as part of your self-instructional material. Of course, replies need not be restricted to written notes or mental considerations; you can ask your learners to perform actions. Self-instructional materials have been designed that ask the learner to conduct interviews as part of data gathering and subsequent analysis, conduct a physical training activity and repair mechanical equipment and to play a musical instrument. In the OU course 'Understanding Music', students developed their keyboard skills through a series of exercises (Example 3.5).

Furthermore, apart from the music example, a learner's reply to the tasks posed in an activity does not necessarily have to be silent. The increased availability of cassette tape recorders and access to both recording and playback facilities provides the opportunity for learners both to hear instructions as well as to record their comments, performance or whatever. A major benefit of hearing the instructions is that the learner's attention, eyes and hands, can concentrate upon the task in hand. For example, an early OU science foundation course (Open University, 1979b) gave an opportunity for students to complete experiments in their own home. They were provided with all the equipment, chemicals and directions they needed to perform the experiment (see Example 3.6). During the experiment students were directed to an audio cassette tape which commented upon the chemical reaction that had taken place – *whilst their eyes were free to concentrate on the result of the reaction.* An extract from the tape is given below:

> What happened when you added the sodium hydroxide solution? Well, you should have got a messy looking reddish brown precipitate. Did you decide what it is? You know that both sodium hydroxide and ferric nitrate are very soluble in water so it can't be either of these. That leaves ferric hydroxide or sodium nitrate as possibilities. Now, you know that most sodium salts are soluble and sodium nitrate is no exception... like most other nitrates it dissolves readily in water so the solid product must be ferric hydroxide, and if your car is as rusty as mine you probably guessed the precipitate contained iron (Open University, 1979b, tape extract).

If the activity calls upon the learner to record a comment, an exchange, sound sequence or whatever, it could be forwarded to a tutor (with obvious delay in feedback) or compared with a recording prepared centrally, requiring the learner to compare and contrast the two. Again the use of an audio cassette tape is probably limited only by your imagination. Self-recorded audio cassette tape has been used to obtain a detailed account of how students perceive and use activities in self-instructional texts (Kaikumba and Cryer, 1987; Lockwood, 1989c). It has also been used to provide feedback on assignments (Knapper, 1980) and to invite learners to respond on tape to recorded comments on their assignments (Evans, 1984).

g. How much time is allocated for the completion of activities?

I suspect that when you were asked to consider how much time is allocated for the completion of activities, it struck you as an odd question. Surely, the time would vary from a few moments reflection to several hours depending upon the task in question; activities would be allocated the amount of time they deserve and require – or would they? The reason for posing the question is associated with exploratory discussions I had several years ago with writers, discussions I have had subsequently on numerous occasions with other writers who have repeatedly confirmed covert institutional practices.

One writer, who had previously confirmed the central place of activities in the teaching text, subsequently identified and described a dilemma facing many authors with regard to the amount of time allocated to an activity in particular and to activities overall. He explained:

Example 3.5 *Playing a melody* (Open University, 1992)

EXERCISE

You might try to clap the rhythm of this, making sure that your two quavers fit exactly into one crotchet. Then, try to play this melody on your keyboard, starting with the thumb of your right hand on the first note. Listen to it again on the cassette. Then play it again on the keyboard.

When you have this fluently under your fingertips, try it starting with your middle finger: this will be helpful later when you progress to melodies with more notes.

Here is the tune an octave higher. Play it on your keyboard several times, starting with the thumb and with your middle finger.

Example 2

Now try playing the tune with your left hand. Again, try it in two ways: starting with your little finger; and then using your middle one, as the point of departure. Here it is, written in the bass clef:

Example 3

Finally, try copying out this tune once or twice to give yourself some writing practice. You will probably want to refer to Sections 3 and 5 of Unit 3 if your writing skills have become a little rusty.

Example 3.6 *Chemical equilibrium* (Open University, 1979b)

Le Chatelier's principle

back at the discussion of acids and bases in Section 2.3. In particular, remember that the net neutralization reaction between an acid and a base is as follows:

$$H^+(aq) + OH^-(aq) = H_2O \qquad (8)$$

Check your ideas by listening to the second part of the tape now.

Part 3

(a) Using a dosing pipette, add not more than five drops of your potassium thiocyanate solution to the second half of your ferric nitrate solution (that is, the half that you did *not* use in part 2 of this experiment). The solution should turn an orange-red colour. You are not expected to interpret this change. The red colour is caused by a complex ion, the ferrithiocyanate ion $(FeSCN)^{2+}$ *, formed by reaction between ferric ions and thiocyanate ions (hence the name): the balanced equation is

$$Fe^{3+}(aq) + SCN^-(aq) \rightleftharpoons (FeSCN)^{2+}(aq) \qquad (18)$$

(b) Now add a few more drops of your KSCN solution. Try to interpret what happens.

(c) Divide the solution obtained in (b) in two by pouring half of it into another test-tube. Using the syringe, add about 1 cm^3 of NaOH solution to one half (mark this A) and then add an equivalent amount of water to the other (mark this B). Compare the two tubes. Try to interpret your observations.

Now listen to the last part of the tape and then try the following ITQs.

* Note that this is a complex cation, which contains a metal atom, iron; other complex ions that you have met so far have contained only non-metals.

ITQ 3   Explain in your own words what happened when you added a few drops of dilute hydrochloric acid to tube A

ITQ 4   Silver thiocyanate, AgSCN, is only very slightly soluble in water. Suppose you have an equilibrium mixture of Fe^{3+} (aq), SCN$^-$ (aq) and (FeSCN)$^{2+}$ (aq) as in part 3a of your experiment. What do you expect to happen if you now add silver nitrate solution? Explain your prediction.

In Home Experiment 2, you have seen how the equilibrium position in a simple chemical system adjusts to changes in the concentrations of reactants or products. Effects like this were studied by the French chemist, Henri Louis Le Chatelier, during the second half of the nineteenth century. (Remember the quotation in the Introduction to this Unit.) Le Chatelier began his career as a mining engineer, but he eventually became Professor of Chemistry at the Sorbonne in 1907. In 1884 he formulated a generalization, based on the results of many observations of chemical equilibria. His generalization has become known as *Le Chatelier's principle*; it can be formulated as follows:

When a system in equilibrium is subjected to an external constraint, the system responds in such a way as to tend to lessen the effect of the constraint.

In the systems you studied in Home Experiment 2, *the external constraint* was the addition, or removal, of reactant or product. However, in the television programme for this Unit, TV 14, you will see that changing other factors (for example, the temperature) can produce similar effects. Time and again in this and the subsequent Unit, you will find that Le Chatelier's principle is invaluable as a qualitative guide to what will happen when an equilibrium system is thrown off balance by changing one or other of these factors.

Now summarize in your own words the main points of Section 3 and then compare your summary with the one in Section 3.5.

Home Experiment 2

To do the experiment you will need the following items from your Home Experiment Kit, Part 2:

Apparatus*
100 cm^3 beaker
100 cm^3 measuring cylinder
rack of test-tubes
5 cm^3 syringe
2 dosing pipettes†
wash-bottle containing distilled water
spatula

Chemicals
sodium hydroxide
dilute hydrochloric acid (8.9%ₐ)
ferric nitrate (iron(III) nitrate)
potassium thiocyanate

Part 1

(a) Using your measuring cylinder, measure 50 cm^3 of distilled water into a beaker and add five pellets of sodium hydroxide, NaOH. Allow to dissolve.

(b) Add enough ferric nitrate, Fe(NO$_3$)$_3$, to a test-tube until the rounded bottom is full. Add enough distilled water to half-fill the test-tube, and shake until the solid dissolves.

(c) Add one crystal of potassium thiocyanate, KSCN, to a test-tube and add enough distilled water to half-fill it. Again shake to dissolve.

All three solutions are ionic. Note the colour of each solution and try to decide which ions are present: record these in Table 2.

TABLE 2 Observations for part 1 of Home Experiment 2

Solid	Colour of solution	Ions present
sodium hydroxide, NaOH		
ferric nitrate, Fe(NO$_3$)$_3$		
potassium thiocyanate, KSCN		

Now listen to the first part of the tape.

Part 2

(a) Divide your ferric nitrate solution in two by pouring half of it into another test-tube. Using the syringe, add about 2 cm^3 of your sodium hydroxide solution to one half. Let this tube stand for a couple of minutes. Explain what you observe by writing a balanced equation, equation 17, for the reaction in the space below.   (17)

(b) Using a dosing pipette, add about ten drops of your dilute hydrochloric acid to the same tube. Shake the tube to mix and then note down your observations. Try to interpret what happens. You will find it is helpful to look

* All the glassware should be clean. Make sure by washing it thoroughly with distilled water.

† Remember not to use the same pipette for transferring different solutions unless you have first washed it. You should also make sure that your spatula is clean and dry.

If I'm absolutely honest you have a systematic interest, as someone writing course material, in underestimating how long activities will take.

If realistic time allocations are provided it reduces the time available to discuss or introduce other aspects of the topic thus reducing the scope and depth of the treatment provided. This colleague believed that many writers experienced this dilemma; a dilemma that can be resolved:

> … if you persuade yourself that activities aren't going to take very long that means students can spend more time on [other aspects of the topic].

If this dilemma is shared by a group of writers it could result in a tacit agreement not to press for realistic time allocations, lest they be applied to everyone's material. Indeed, the likelihood of such an agreement was implied by the writer when commenting upon a particular time allocation for one of his activities:

> … the time seems to be hopelessly inadequate, fifteen minutes, if you look at the questions I've been asking… fifteen minutes is scandalous and it's scandalous that I didn't appreciate that and it's probably scandalous that the rest of the course team didn't as well, that we as a community didn't.

It may be worth looking again at some of your activities, or those designed by colleagues. Do they represent realistic time allocations or not? Has time been 'shaved off' to allow other materials to be included?

Concluding comments

I trust the above activity and comments were useful in helping you distinguish between your espoused theories concerning the role of activities in texts and your theories-in-use. If they enable you to identify design practices that you and your colleagues employ and to begin the process of assessing their effectiveness, then this chapter has fulfilled its purpose. Of course, an honest assessment of the way you design activities and awareness of your assumptions does not guarantee that your learners will perceive and use them in the way you expect. Indeed, many writers have acknowledged their ignorance of how activities are actually used. The following remark is typical:

> I don't know how they're using them. . . you assume they're using them the way you've set them up and part of the problem of course is that numbers of students don't do activities or they do them selectively using priorities that you don't know.

Others have speculated upon how learners do interact with the activities and have suggested that:

> ... the traditional role is to look at them, to read them and perhaps think about a part of it but then to be more interested in what you say about it than actually taking the required amount of time you've specified. I should imagine about a handful of students might actually do that, but the majority of them not... I would hope that most students would get something out of them.

Such statements may be accurate reflections. However, there is every likelihood that these sentiments will be communicated to colleagues, contribute to the group's ongoing socialization within the institution and influence their assumptions regarding student use of activities. Indeed, it is possible that these assumptions could contribute to a self-fulfilling prophecy. If authors believe students use activities in the way described above, then decisions to bury them in the text without a time allocation or to allocate less time would be a pragmatic solution to the constraints under which authors are working and the way in which students work. As a result, an insight into how students perceive and use activities is essential; it is the focus of the next chapter.

Chapter 4

What do learners think about activities?

Associated benefits and costs

If learners are to respond to an activity along the lines suggested, and in the time suggested by a writer, they must have some incentive or reason for doing so. Equally, if a learner decides not to respond to an activity there must be some reason for this. If we can identify what these reasons are we will be better able to understand the influences upon a learner and to share this knowledge with all concerned.

Note that I am not suggesting that a knowledge of the reasons why learners do not complete activities is the basis for some ploy or tactic to manipulate or coerce them. The assumptions held by writers, described in the previous chapter and elsewhere (Gibbs et al, 1982), indicate there is still a tendency to regard the task of writing self-instructional material as one of carefully controlling the way individuals learn. The logical structuring of texts and the strategic inclusion of activities to control learning is regarded by many as an admirable goal. However, research into what learners do when they study self-instructional material (see, for example Duchastel and Whitehead, 1980; Lockwood, 1989b; Nathenson, 1978) suggests that control may be unattainable, that numerous factors combine to influence how an individual is likely to respond to an activity.

Let's return to the point about the reasons why an individual may decide to respond to an activity or not. From your experience as a teacher, trainer, writer of self-instructional material or simply as someone who has studied self-instructional material, what do you think could be the benefits that a learner hopes to obtain from completing an activity? From the comments so far it would be reasonable for a learner to regard the activity as contributing to their understanding of the course content, the particular ideas, relationships, procedures and techniques that are at the centre of the teaching; benefits that are focused upon the content of the course. What other benefits do you think an activity might provide? In Activity 4.1 I've offered this possible benefit as an illustration and invite you to spend a few minutes reflecting upon what other benefits you can identify and to jot them down.

ACTIVITY 4.1 Benefits provided by activities

What are the benefits that you feel a learner may associate with the completion of activities? Trying to identify these is an opportunity to consider the benefits of activities as perceived by a learner.

If possible try to group the benefits you identify in a meaningful way (meaningful to you) and give them a descriptive label. An example is given to start you off.

Course-focused benefits
1. Those related to learning from the course – the concepts, ideas, arguments, procedures, techniques, etc. that contribute to their understanding of or their mastery of the topic(s) under consideration

2.

3.

What other benefits did you identify? Were you able to group them in any meaningful way and give them a descriptive label?

On the basis of studies I've conducted with OU students, and which I have confirmed with other groups of learners, I would like to describe three major benefits that learners claim and which I have placed in three separate categories: course-focused benefits, self- focused benefits and assignment-focused benefits. After reading a description of them, illustrated by typical quotes from learners, you can then decide the extent to which they relate to the ones you have identified and which your learners may perceive.

Course-focused benefits

Course-focused benefits, as indicated above, are those that relate to learning from a course or topic; the concepts, ideas, arguments under discussion, the techniques, procedures or skills being practised. For learners in this category, the activities are perceived as contributing to their understanding of the material. A typical comment from a learner would be:

> If it looks like it is going to tie in and it is going to increase my understanding later in the course... then I will work through it very, very methodically.

Whilst this comment indicates a broad or generalized course-focused benefit, that an activity offers more specific course-focused benefits may be recognized. For example, activities can be regarded as,

> … helpful in concentrating your thinking on the major points that have been covered… I assume that they've been put in to help you see that which is important in the work you've just covered and so I take them as a guideline for that.

This narrowing of the focus, from a general to a more restricted one is evident in many comments from learners. For example, activities provide these benefits because, '… [they] give you a greater insight into the concepts of the course … encourage one to pause and reflect…'.

Activities can also provide opportunities for the learner to practice certain techniques or skills. These can include, for example, interview techniques used in market research and ways of analysing statistical data to handing specialist equipment, conducting experiments and developing manipulative skills.

> I can see that I'll need to be able to do that whilst 'waiting' [silver service skills] and so it's worth practising.

> Until I tried it I thought it didn't matter how you did it [fault-finding in electronic equipment] but I can now see that [the procedure they recommend] makes sense and will help in future.

Self-focused benefits

Self-focused benefits are those that relate to one's learning and development as a person; the opportunities they provide for ideas and arguments to be explored or reconsidered, previous assumptions challenged and personal interest awakened, developed or extended. For learners in this category, activities are,

> Beneficial to me personally… to expand the knowledge that I have and perhaps push me into areas that I might not have thought about … trying to introduce other aspects, materials that I might not otherwise think of using.

The challenge that activities provided for these individuals is reflected in the following comment in which activities enabled one to,

> … analyse your thoughts a bit more instead of just reading line after line. They say stop and just go back and just think about what you have read and in putting it in a different way make you think.

The central feature of those comments categorized as self-focused is one of thinking critically, of questioning the materials, challenging assumptions and previous ideas. The following quotes express this clearly:

> I assume that the rationale behind [activities] is to make it perhaps clear to you what assumptions you had or have which you might possibly wish to reconsider.

> ... the activities are just trying to make you take a wider stance and ... think more openly about it and to question your own thinking and to probe your thinking and to probe your own view point.

Assignment-focused benefits

Assignment-focused benefits are those that contribute directly to answering a test or some other form of assignment, that provide an opportunity to either think about the issues to be discussed or which provide materials to be used in it. Learners within this category remark,

> ... it depends on how much it would relate to the assignment because that's the way I work and if I think that this is going to get me thinking more clearly about the issues at stake in the assignment then I might attempt it.

> ... if it's relevant to the [assignment] and if I feel I can use it, I would definitely do it ... and do it properly... I won't do anything unless it's totally relevant to getting a good grade.

Learners who perceive assignment-focused benefits often flag those activities they feel are potentially relevant to answering an assignment question: 'I put marks by those if I think that's particularly relevant to the assignment... I do find [them] useful for that'.

Some learners actually return to particular activities whilst assembling their assignment:

> ... when I come to the essays... I find myself going back to an activity and actually having another close look at that because... some part [provides] assistance in helping to answer the question.

The above constructs emerged during detailed analyses of interview transcripts, self-recorded audio tapes and written questionnaires (Lockwood, 1990). They were also informed by the work of several researchers, in particular Mathias (1980) who had undertaken qualitative research into attitudes and approaches to study. During Mathias' research two major approaches to study were identified and termed 'course-focused (CF)' and 'interest-focused (IF)'. A CF approach to study was characterized by students placing emphasis on competence as a basis for interest in their study; any set or voluntary study was exclusively within the framework of the course. Those students adopting an IF approach to study placed emphasis on interest in the material as a basis for competence. Voluntary study extended beyond the confines of the course and was dictated by students' own interests and preferences. In this context the construct course-focused benefits has similarities with Mathias' CF approach and self-focused benefits with Mathias' IF.

It is interesting to note that although Mathias did not identify an assignment-focused approach amongst the students in his study – one equivalent to the assignment-focused benefits – various remarks by Mathias indicate it could have been identified. Indeed, during an account of his research Mathias notes that amongst student comments, '… there were striking similarities with the notion of "cue consciousness"' (Mathias, 1980, p 50). (The concept of 'cue consciousness' [Miller and Parlett, 1974] seeks to explain the influence of course assessment upon the strategies that learners adopt towards assignments.) However, Mathias incorporated aspects that may have been associated with an assignment-focused approach within the CF approach.

Costs

So much for the benefits that may be associated with completing activities; but what about the costs? What costs do you think most learners believe they incur whilst responding to an activity? Certainly, all the indicators from existing research (see Duchastel and Whitehead, 1980; Henderson, 1977; Kaye, 1972) and evidence I've collected (Lockwood, 1990) are that the benefits provided by activities are balanced by a major cost – the study time that they consume; it pervades virtually all learner comments:

I rarely go anywhere near the time that you are supposed to spend on [activities] … you are under too much pressure to do that.

… it takes too much time, it becomes time-consuming and the extra time involved, very often, I don't think is justified.

I don't really have time … I'll do what I think necessary and leave it at that … There never seems to be enough time.

I don't spend as much time [on activities] as I should.

I don't do all of them, it depends again on time.

Time must be part of the answer. If I feel I am under a sort of pressure.

Activity 4.2 gives you the opportunity to reflect on your experience and to identify those additional costs that you feel your learners may associate with activities or which they may incur while attempting them. Identifying these costs may enable you to better understand the process that your learners are engaged in.

If no other costs immediately spring to mind consider the assumptions and expectations you listed in Activity 3.1 on p.00 and consider emotional as well as intellectual costs. As in Activity 4.1, try to group any of the costs you identify and give them a descriptive label.

ACTIVITY 4.2 Costs associated with activities

What are the costs that learners may associate with activities? These may be intellectual, emotional or practical. An example is given to start you off.

1. *Consumed study time*
   Responding to activities takes valuable study time that could be given to other tasks within the course.
2.

3.

What other costs did you identify? Did you manage to group them in a meaningful way and give them a descriptive label?

I can imagine a series of practical costs associated with activities, like physically coordinating all the materials that may be needed to complete an activity: gaining access to a cassette tape recorder, video playback equipment, the apparatus for some experiment or workplace in which to complete the task set. However, careful flagging of the text enables learners to note what other materials, resources or context are needed so that they can phase their study and be in the appropriate place or have the necessary material to hand. (I can also imagine the practical problems faced by the partially sighted, those with impaired hearing or physical disabilities. Unfortunately a discussion of the provision of large print or Braille materials, transcripts, etc. for disabled learners is inappropriate here but could well be an issue for you and your colleagues.)

During interviews, analysis of questionnaires and discussion with learners, from a variety of contexts, I have identified three potential costs which I've called *degradation*, *deference* and *inadequacy* and which illustrate intellectual and emotional costs. These are briefly outlined below; they are described and illustrated in more detail in the next section.

Degradation – in an attempt to save study time many learners simply read through the activity and follow-up comment with little or no attempt to respond to it; they focus upon the product of the activity rather than the process it embodies. Alternatively, they grossly simplify the task, making it less demanding and less time-consuming than originally intended. In both cases learners incur an intellectual cost to their study by degrading the activity.

Deference – after assembling their own response to an activity and looking at the writer's follow-up comment, learners display undue deference by discarding their own response in favour of that offered by the writer, even when the intention of the writer is to encourage learners to think for themselves and have confidence in the case they had assembled. Learners incur an intellectual cost to their study when they fail to appreciate the legitimacy of a relativistic conception of knowledge (Perry, 1970).

Inadequacy – an emotional cost is incurred by learners when, as a result of not completing activities to save study time, they acquire feelings of guilt and inadequacy. These feelings are generated through recognition of the benefits that the activities provide, and a belief that they have a valuable role to play in their study, but not availing themselves of them.

It is interesting to note that in his investigation of student approaches to study, Mathias described students as developing strategies towards their study which enabled them not merely to cope with the course but to survive. For some students he remarked,

> Their perceived inability to cope gave rise to some degree of frustration and demoralisation, a questioning of their abilities and a reassessment of their degree and career hopes (Mathias, 1980, p 44).

This description, in the context of learners commenting on their perception and use of activities, is similar to the cost identified as 'inadequacy'.

I trust you found the description of the above costs plausible. However, I suspect that you are also of the opinion that not all learners will incur all of these costs. It is likely that some do not degrade activities: they complete them along the lines suggested and in the general time suggested by the writer. Some, rather than displaying deference to writers' follow-up comments and discarding their initial responses, are likely to have confidence in their own viewpoint or ideas. Similarly, not all learners will feel guilty or inadequate about not completing activities. They may regard activities as a resource and their role one of deciding which of the available resources to draw upon. Completing some and not others would be consistent with being an effective and efficient learner. Finally, it is possible that some learners are not preoccupied with saving study time and they are happy to spend time on activities.

In recognition of this possibility, supported by analysis of learners' comments, the costs identified as degradation, deference and inadequacy need to be balanced by corresponding benefits as indicated in Figure 4.1 and described in the next section. Furthermore, from the above comments, the single cost associated with consumed study time would be more appropriately represented as two categories: one associated with study time savers (those trying to save study time by the various methods described above) and one with study time spenders (those who do spend time on the various activities).

Figure 4.1 *Constructs describing the costs and benefits associated with activities in self-instructional texts*

- Degradation – Completion
- Deference – Confidence
- Inadequacy – Efficiency
- Study time savers – Study time spenders

Description of costs and benefits

Each of the constructs that have been identified are described below and illustrated by typical quotes from learners. Whilst reading through them you can decided the extent to which your learners could be described in similar ways.

Degradation – Completion

One of the expectations of writers is that in responding to the various intellectual demands embodied in the activities, learners will think about the course material and the issues involved, and relate these to their previous understanding and perhaps revise their original ideas or views. Some learners do respond to activities in this way. Indeed, completion of activities along the lines suggested by the writer is consistent with the categorization of learners as perceiving course-focused, self-focused and assignment-focused benefits. The following comments are typical of those learners categorized as completing activities and represent the completion category of this construct.

I always do them and do them properly 'cos they're an important part of the course. If the author wants you to compare one view with another, think about the argument... sort out your ideas or whatever it's because it's an important part of studying.

It's possible to skip the activities but if you do you're missing a great opportunity to think through your ideas and sort them out... to analyse things, offer your interpretation.

Many learners, while maybe not completing an activity along the lines suggested and in the time suggested by the writer, do give it some thought before proceeding to the follow-up comment; they can be judged to be completing activities. For example,

I don't... always put anything down on paper. I will often construct the idea in my mind and they help me to lay out what I think – so they are important.

... it depends entirely on the activity. Some of them I just look at and do in my head, sometimes I just get a piece of paper and scribble a few notes, other times I am more extensive – it depends what is asked for.

In contrast to learners who complete activities along the lines suggested, many reduce the demands or degrade them; they reduce the intellectual demands of an activity thus making it simpler than intended and less time-consuming than expected. Often the demands of the activity are recognized by students but substituted for less taxing ones. The following comments are typical and represent the degradation category of the first construct identified as Degradation – Completion:

They're wanting you to analyse the argument in the reading – I haven't got time for that so I just read through to get an idea of what they're saying and thought about it a bit before continuing.

It asked you to compare the different views and assess the strengths and weaknesses of the two... I didn't bother... I just read them and decided which one was closest to my own view and why.

Comments from learners indicate that despite the careful wording and explanation accompanying an activity they are often interpreted as requiring much simpler replies than intended. For example, an activity that asked a learner to evaluate an argument, considering a series of points in turn and the extent to which they are supported or refuted was reduced to a memory list: 'I tried to spot two or three important points and remember them'.

Learners also collapsed the question(s) and associated follow-up comments that constitute an activity into a continuation of the text – focusing on the product of the activity rather than the process, making little or no attempt to formulate a response and thus reducing its intellectual demands. The following comment is typical:

> I won't actually get down to doing it [answering the questions in the activity] because I have got a better comment underneath. We're mere mortals and undergraduates know that you blokes have got the best comment so we take yours. You might as well spend ten minutes learning that as sorting your own out.

A similar comment is provided by a learner who maintained she just,

> ... read the comment... because you know it's one way again of cutting down the time and it's all written in the comment anyway so I can't really see the point of slogging through it.

Degrading activities also had the effect of reducing or eliminating the excitement that writers are trying to achieve in their teaching. For example, a learner remarked:

> I didn't... give it a chance to surprise me, I just looked, read through that [the question] and I read through that [follow-up] straight away.

Deference – Confidence

A learner's desire to comprehend the material being presented, to understand the ideas or arguments offered by the writer, is a fundamental part of study. In study areas new to a person it is not unreasonable to assume that learners will credit a writer with experience, academic competence and skill superior to their own and, in the absence of other authorities, will accept writers' interpretations, analyses, conclusions and recommendations.

However, many writers maintained they are not merely providing academic or technical content and opportunities for learners to check their understanding but opportunities to challenge previous conceptions, to engage with the material and, above all, to think for themselves. The fostering of learner independence is a major objective of many writers and the activities a mechanism to realize it.

Activities that merely require recall, comprehension or limited interpretation provide little opportunity for learners to formulate a response that can differ legitimately from a writer. However, activities that provide scope for learners to formulate responses that can differ significantly from the view offered by the writer, and which are equally valid, provide such an opportunity. Some learners grasp these opportunities and have confidence in their own response. This confidence may be regarded as an intellectual benefit of completing activities and one category of this second construct. The following comments are typical of confident learners.

I have got my own opinion about it – he has got his. Then I will probably think 'Well, why did he get his and I get mine the way it is?'

… if I think that mine are just as valuable as his comments then I will keep them… I don't just say 'Oh, that's it, I have got it wrong!'

… It's not a case of right or wrong but the balance of the arguments one wants to take and the emphasis you want to give. Quite often I disagree with the way the author has argued his case – stressing some points and omitting others… so I am just not prepared to accept what he says unless I can see the strength of his argument against the alternative.

I don't regard the [comments on] activities as 'tablets of stone'… I think they are to be questioned and if they are doing their job properly we ought to be questioning them and if we are doing our job properly there ought to be questioning.

[When] we've got a difference of opinion … you've got to respect both … because there's no one way of thinking about many of these things in these units, there can be lots of ways of thinking about them. [I wouldn't merely accept a writer's comment] … if I could justify mine.

In contrast to those learners who display confidence in the arguments they marshal there are others who, upon discovering their initial response or reaction to an activity differed from the writer's, abandoned their own and adopt the writer's, without exploring the value of the activity, attempting to resolve the difference of opinion, as those above had done. They can be categorized as displaying deference to writers' comments at the expense of their own as illustrated below:

If [my own answer] differed I usually choose the author's and change mine to suit … I usually end up taking the author's answers in place of my own… when it comes to revision I would not remember what was right and what was wrong.

If it is … because … I have reached the wrong conclusions … made an incorrect analysis [would change response] I would not expect to get them all right … that's his greater experience which I haven't got. If I had been cleverer… that's what I would have put.

There is still the innate feeling that those in authority… must know what they're doing … I know I shouldn't but I still tend to believe that the author will be right … I automatically … feel I must be wrong.

Others explained their reaction when their response was different from the author's:

I feel rather unnerved… I sort of put it down as though I have put it in my answer when in fact I have not. It is a childish tendency to think 'I have failed. Quick, I must put that down and pretend I had it' and I do that. I can see myself doing that … because I am prepared to accept the person who is giving the comment is giving me some sort of 'right answer'.

Inadequacy – Efficiency

An emotional implication of learners' failure to complete activities along the lines suggested by the writer is that many of them regard themselves as inadequate; they regard themselves as poor learners who are not doing themselves justice in their study, not getting from the course all they could. These feelings of guilt and inadequacy can be represented by an inadequacy category within the Inadequacy – Efficiency construct. Learners incurring this emotional cost are aware of the potential role of activities in their study and make remarks like:

Oh, [the activity] aids your understanding, it certainly does… and I'm a fool to myself for not doing them.

I thought they were all worthwhile, it's a great shame that I just haven't got the time to give to them.

I'd taken the lazy way out and not done it… I'm beginning to think I'm rather lazy… I'm not taking advantage of the activities.

I'd only use the ones I think were going to be relevant [to the assignment] … I think this is why I'm such a bad student because I know I shouldn't do that. I should read them all … it's terrible to admit this.

When learners are asked what their reaction would be if activities were omitted from future self-instructional material, a typical response was that they would feel relieved (a word repeated by many learners); it would remove the feeling of guilt or inadequacy they experienced when skimming over or ignoring them.

For some learners the decision to complete some activities, ignore others or to complete them less thoroughly than is suggested is regarded as a legitimate strategy if they are to perform as effective and efficient learners. They believe that they are expected to study selectively since the course materials are a resource for them to draw upon. Learners who demonstrate efficiency, as a result of their selective study of course materials, may be regarded as the other category of the construct. The following comments are typical:

> There's so much in the course that one has to be selective… I am sure they don't expect you to read every word and do every activity… part of being an undergraduate is deciding what areas to follow up, what activities can be skipped and those you need to do – using your time to best effect.

> It depends on people's background, if one's background is such that you've never come across a particular concept then you would probably like to spend more time on it, and some activities that I find very difficult I'm sure that other people would find really easy and therefore wouldn't have to spend time on them.

> I don't think you're expected to do all the activities… they are there merely to help you if you need them.

> Some people might get quite a bit from doing activities but for the ones that don't do, well, it's something they can miss out – like I do so that I have time to do other areas that I feel are more important.

> … I think there have to be some areas left to the decision of the student.

Study time savers – study time spenders

Previous comments have indicated that concern over available study time pervades virtually all learner comments. However, not all learners skip or degrade activities to save time; some, in the process of their study, spend valuable time on them. The allocation of study time can be regarded as a fourth construct. A learner for whom the study time consumed outweighed the benefits they offered can be categorized as a study time saver, who would:

> Look at it and think 'have I got time?'… I am under pressure and if I am then I'll just ignore it completely and if I'm not I'll look at it and think 'is it worth tackling or not?'

> If I feel that I am a bit pushed for time … the things that tend to go by

Figure 4.2 *Perception of activities in texts; a cost-benefit analysis model*

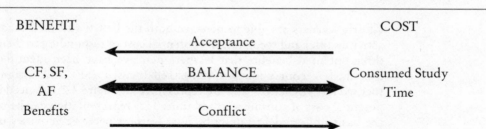

the board are the little activities … they tend to be the things that are skimped over.

Such learners may be of the opinion that activities '… can hinder study if they slow you down… study time is so precious'. For others, even potentially valuable activities are discarded because of time pressures: '… I didn't do [the activity] really for lack of time rather than it not being a good activity'.

In the other category of this construct are those learners who distribute their available study time over all elements in the teaching material – including the activities. These learners spend as long on the activities as they need to avail themselves of the benefits they offer; they are identified as study time spenders. The following comments are typical:

I don't have all the time in the world but I do try and spread my time over all the bits in the course – including the activities. I spend as long on them as I need to make sure I understand what it's all about. Sometimes I take longer than they say, sometimes shorter … I don't really clock watch.

I'm not guided by the amount of time it says… I spent a lot of time on that [activity] and then … a lot more time thinking of things after I read that comment … [I] spend as much time as I think is useful upon them.

I think the vast majority of them I have worked through.
I generally enjoy the activities and often spend more than the 5 – 10 minutes that they say.

Conflict, acceptance and balance – a cost-benefit analysis model

Clearly learners are able to perceive both the benefits to their study that activities offer and recognize the potential cost of responding to them. The three potential benefits that learners perceive have been identified and described – course-focused (CF), self-focused (SF) and assignment-focused (AF) benefits – and are represented in Figure 4.2, balanced by the potential cost of consumed study time. This representation can be used as the basis of a model to describe how learners perceive activities in self-instructional material – a cost-benefit analysis model. (Not to be confused with the cost-benefit analysis model used in economics in which all the elements are related to a financial measure and which often entails great ingenuity in quantifying the various constituent elements and reducing them to monetary terms.)

When learners reconcile the benefits offered by activities with the costs they are likely to incur in responding to them, they operate a cost-benefit analysis. My own research suggests that the vast majority of learners operate a balance – responding to some activities and not others as study time pressures and the perceived value of benefits vary. This balance is a central feature and is represented in the middle of Figure 4.2 by a thick two-way arrow in which large arrow heads point towards both the benefits and the costs, signifying that benefits are obtained but at a cost. However, for some learners the task is perceived as either resolving a conflict between the demands of activities and available study time or acceptance of the activities as an integral part of the teaching. In a conflict situation activities are virtually ignored; this is represented in the bottom half of Figure 4.2 by a single arrow in which the head points towards the cost of completing activities and away from the benefits they provide. Where acceptance is the characteristic, virtually every activity is completed along the lines suggested by the author. This is signified by an arrow pointing away from the cost, in terms of consumed study time, and towards the benefits available.

However, there is a distinction between perceiving the potential benefits of activities in texts and availing oneself of them. Students may be aware of what the author is trying to do in the activities but simply not prepared to respond to them, or they respond to them selectively.

Despite the constant pressure upon available study time the evidence from surveys, interviews and discussions indicates that a majority of learners are prepared to expend time on activities. They take the middle course between spending time to complete some activities and ignoring others because of the cost of consumed study time. This balance, this preparedness to devote at least some of their valuable study time to activities, is evident in the following comments:

That particular one I didn't do, I was very naughty. I'll be honest, that one I didn't do really from lack of time rather than it not being a good activity ... I may well come back to it.

... it all depends on the time factor. If I have got enough time ... I will probably do more of the activity because I have got more time to study it.

Well, it all depends on the amount of time I have ... I have a little look at what activities are on offer ... make a mental note of the ones I might do and the ones I might not ... depending on how much time I've got.

I always make a conscious decision... even if I don't decide to do it... it depends entirely on the activity.

Some learners feel under so much pressure that the time demanded for activities conflicts with other study tasks and results in their virtual omission from study. For example, such learners remark:

Once I have geared myself up to not bothering too much about the activities, which I must admit I haven't bothered much with, I just do the reading.

I don't do them. Well, I read them but I'm still behind ... I can't, I haven't got time for that, I'm behind ... it's habit now of not doing them and I didn't do them last year either.

I'd never dream of sitting down and answering them on paper ... I glance at them. Think, I think quickly about them and go straight on. I would never do them I don't think, no I wouldn't.

I don't consider the exercises, for want of a better word, very important because your ideas, or the [writer's] are written down there anyway and I vaguely know my own thoughts on things without putting them into words, without thinking too deeply.

Some learners complete virtually all activities along the lines suggested by the writer; they are accepted as a central part of the teaching material. For example, such learners remark:

I try and answer the activities of course ... I found that writing them out is taking a very long time so I sometimes just think out the activities rather than ... writing them out. I don't always time it. I take whatever time I need to finish it.

Activities are completed as they appear, then ... [I] compare work with the author's.

I do the activities… I write it down and I do it, it's just a habit I've got into… I accept it as part of the ritual of doing the course.

I will do the ones I can do, activity wise, once or twice in the past I've… left [an activity] out… it's only happened once or twice… other than that I've always carefully written down the answer and waited until the end to see if my answers tally or not.

For these learners, the consumed study time is seen as a reasonable cost, if it is considered at all.

However, an indication that the decision regarding the role of activities in self-instructional material may not be a clear one is illustrated by the comments from one learner that I interviewed. This man made repeated and favourable references towards activities, saying '… they're very good… helpful… well worthwhile… helpful in concentrating your thinking… all worthwhile'. His reaction to their absence from subsequent teaching material appeared genuine. He said 'I'd miss them… they are a help as far as I'm concerned… I'd be disappointed [if omitted from the teaching]'. However, despite these assertions and recognition of their potential value, '…I assume that they've been put in to help you see that which is important in the work you've just covered'. They played a minor role in his study. He professed to be extremely slow at studying and explained, '… having fallen behind I can't afford… I've got to make cuts and that's [completing activities] where I choose to make them'. The dilemma facing this learner typifies the central feature of balancing or resolving conflict associated with the opportunities provided by study and the implications associated with it. Availing oneself of the benefits offered by activities, whether they be course-, self- or assignment-focused, has a cost, or rather a series of potential costs.

Further consideration of the cost-benefit analysis model suggests that the above constructs can be described in terms of four features:

a. the cost of responding to activities;
b. the benefits of responding to activities;
c. the cost of not responding to activities;
d. the benefits of not responding;

and represented diagrammatically in one of four areas (a, b, c, d) of Figure 4.3.

A major intellectual benefit of completing an activity is that learners would be able to avail themselves of those course-focused, self-focused or assignment-focused benefits they perceive. These intellectual benefits can be grouped under the heading, 'Completion of activities' in area b. of Figure 4.3.

Figure 4.3 *Diagrammatic representation of the cost-benefit analysis model*

Effective and efficient

a. Cost of responding
Study time spent

b. Benefits of responding
Completion of activities
Confidence in own
arguments

c. Cost of not responding
Degradation of activities
Deference to authors

d. Benefits of not responding
Study time saved

Guilt and inadequacy

A major intellectual cost of not responding to the activities along the lines suggested by the writer and in the time suggested would be that learners miss the opportunity to explore, refine, challenge or apply the particular ideas, concepts or arguments under discussion. They would incur an intellectual cost by not involving themselves in the processes represented by the activity. Some learners skip entire activities in order to save time and study other parts of the material. Others, while not skipping the activity completely, either focus on the product of the activity rather than the process (they merely studied the writer's follow-up comment rather than engaging in the task posed), or simplify the activity considerably making it less demanding and less time-consuming than intended. This cost is represented in area c. of Figure 4.3 as 'Degradation of activities'

A second major intellectual benefit of completing activities is that learners gain confidence in the arguments they marshal and in views that differ from those of the writer; learners are 'thinking for themselves'. These benefits are represented in area b. of Figure 4.3 under the heading 'Confidence in own arguments'. An intellectual cost of not responding to activities along the lines suggested by the writer, giving them limited attention and not assembling their own arguments to questions posed, is to lack confidence in their own responses. This is illustrated in the deference that learners display to writers' comments at the expense of their own. This cost is represented in area c. of Figure 4.3 under the heading of 'Deference to authors'.

The benefits and cost of responding to activities in terms of the study time consumed can be readily represented in Figure 4.3. The benefit of not responding to an activity is that study time is saved and is thus available for other study tasks. The cost is that study time is spent which cannot be replaced, thus contributing to the pervasive concern regarding the time that study consumes. This is represented in Figure 4.3 under the headings of 'Study time saved' and 'Study time spent'; areas d. and a. respectively.

The emotional cost that many learners incur during their study, as a result of their decision to save study time by not responding to activities, is to acquire feelings of guilt and inadequacy – feelings that the writers I have interviewed did not envisage. Many learners also incur intellectual costs when they degrade activities or display deference to writers' comments. This is represented in Figure 4.3 by the heading 'Guilt and inadequacy' which bridges areas c. and d. The emotional benefit of spending time on selected activities, and having confidence in their own arguments, is to acquire feelings of being an effective and efficient learner. This is represented in Figure 4.3 by the heading 'Effective and efficient' which bridges areas a. and b.

Nature of the cost-benefit analysis model

Within the cost-benefit analysis model several relationships are likely. For example, learners categorized as study time savers are less likely to complete activities along the lines suggested by the writer; they are more likely to degrade activities. If learners do not engage in the process central to an activity they will have little or no information upon which to formulate their own response and hence could be more likely to accept the writers' comments, analysis or argument; to display deference. (Learners may, of course, have a naïve confidence in their previous views and opinions and by not challenging them during an activity may retain confidence in their response.) Since all learners recognize one or more benefits that activities provide, the accumulation of feelings of inadequacy as a result of not availing themselves of these opportunities is plausible.

In contrast, learners categorized as study time spenders are more likely to complete activities along the lines suggested by the writer and obtain the course-focused, self-focused or assignment-focused benefits available. Furthermore, if learners complete the activities they have more likelihood of generating confidence in the arguments they mount or responses they formulate and are less likely to regard themselves as inadequate learners. Indeed, it is plausible that such learners would regard the teaching material as a resource and their selective use of it as demonstrating their efficiency as a learner.

The above explanation is useful but infers a static description of the essentially dynamic processes involved in learners' perception and use of activities. Furthermore, findings from other investigations into student learning (Laurillard, 1978) indicate that learners vary their approach to a task according to their perception of it. Laurillard argued that learning strategies are not fixed but content and context dependent. There is some evidence that the relative position of activities within a unit, the presence or absence of a framework, grid or space in which to record a response, and the method and nature of response required by a student do influence the use of activities; a point considered below.

Learner use of activities

Although activities are a characteristic of self-instructional teaching material there has been little research, in non-experimental settings, into those features that may influence their use. The most recent survey of activities in OU teaching material, now quite old, noted that activities:

> … have a complex status in the eyes of students and that reactions of students to their use … are not likely to form an overall picture which is simple and straightforward (Duchastel and Whitehead, 1980, p 41).

Other colleagues had earlier noted that there was a tendency for learners to think about their response to an activity rather than write it down (Lawless, 1976) and those activities that provided a space or grid for a response were more likely to be completed (Henderson, 1977).

It would appear that in addition to the time likely to be associated with an activity there are at least two other features of activities that have already been identified as possible influences upon a learner's response. One of these can be called an operational influence – whether a learner thinks about a response or performs the suggested task, be this simply writing down a response, completing some experiment or practical exercise. The other can be called typographical – whether a space, grid or framework is provided for a response or whether the learner is expected to create their own.

What other features do you think may influence someone approaching one of your activities, one that you have designed and integrated into your self-instructional material? You may find it useful to look back to some of the activities that you and your colleagues have devised and try to detect those features that may influence learners. In Activity 4.3 I have listed three possible influences – Temporal, Operational and Typographical. I have included temporal (the time that is associated with completing an activity) because previous discussion indicates study time to be a major concern. As such it is possible that the length of time allocated to an activity may have an influence; short activities allocated 2–3 minutes being viewed differently from those allocated 15–20 minutes or more.

ACTIVITY 4.3 Features influencing learners' response to activities

What features, in addition to those already identified as Temporal, Operational and Typographi-cal, do you think are likely to influence a learner's response to an activity? You may find it helpful to look through some existing self-instructional material to detect these possible influences.

When you have identified various possible influences try to group them in a meaningful way and give them a descriptive label like the examples provided.

1. *Temporal* – the time associated with an activity; whether it is brief or lengthy

2. *Operational* – the method of responding to the activity; thinking about it, writing an answer or completing a practical task.

3. *Typographical* – the presence or absence of a framework, grid or space in which to record a response.

4.

5.

What additional features did you identify and have you any evidence to suggest that the features may indeed be influential?

In a study designed to investigate the above features and to detect others (Lockwood, 1990) an example of OU teaching material was identified that was typical of the self-instructional material produced by the School of Education. The material, a multi-media teaching text equivalent to 12–14 hours of study time, contained a variety of activities. These could be readily identified typographically; they were accompanied by both a time allocation and a follow-up comment with several providing a space or grid within which to record a response. While learners were free to respond to the activities in any way, several actually suggested mental and written responses to the questions posed.

A total of 53 students were identified and divided into three sub-samples with questions posed during face-to-face interviews (12 students), by students recording their own comments on audio tape (16 students) and in written replies to questionnaire items (25 students) (Lockwood, 1989c). The questions recorded the level of response to each part of the activities in the teaching text, explored students' reactions to the above features and tried to detect others.

During detailed analyses of questions linked to individual activities in the OU teaching material the influence of the three features mentioned above was confirmed and others identified. The two additional features were called 'Positional' – the relative position of an activity in the teaching material, and 'Intellectual' – the demands made by the activity; recall/comprehension or interpretation/analysis. The actual influence of these features is described below.

Positional: the relative position of an activity in the text

The activities within the OU teaching material were positioned at fairly regular intervals throughout its length. When the proportion of students completing these activities was determined it revealed that students appeared to be more diligent with regard to activities early in their study of the teaching material than towards the end of it, when time pressures increase or come to the fore. The proportion of activities completed dwindled from 90–100 per cent at the start to 30–40 per cent as the teaching text progressed towards the end; extremely similar patterns of response being evident in data collected by the three different methods. In discussion students explained how they commenced their study with good intentions but as they worked through the material, and as study time pressure increased, activities were skipped or skimmed:

> … If I feel I am a bit pushed for time on a particular unit the things that tend to go by the board are the little activities.

> I was slightly behind on my work schedule… I was anxious to get on to the second part of the unit.

> … that particular one I didn't do – really for lack of time rather than it not being a good activity – given the time I may well come back to it.

An inspection of the actual material discussed with students revealed that some of the activities were made up of several questions. For example, one activity asked students to read a particular passage presented in the text, to list different meanings of a term used in the passage and finally to contrast different definitions of this term. In such situations if a student does not respond to the first task posed in an activity it is often difficult, if not impossible, for them to respond to subsequent tasks. Indeed, an analysis of the data revealed that of those activities that posed more than one task, a reduced level of response to subsequent tasks was recorded in the majority of them.

Typographical: the presence or absence of a framework, grid or space in which to record a response

A record of responses to those activities that did and did not provide a framework, grid or space for a response, together with an analysis of student responses to questions posed revealed that the majority of students preferred activities that provided a framework, grid or space within which to record a response – even when they realized that completing the activity was not as easy as they first thought:

> … If I see a grid and I have got to put a tick or a cross, yes, I will do that.

> I'm much more likely to do an activity if there is space on the paper for me to write what is asked for.

> … where you can go through and tick particular things or making little comments alongside – I will often do those because there is a space to actually do it.

Further analysis also revealed that when a grid or framework was provided for a simple response, like a tick or a cross, extremely large proportions – 80–100 per cent – of learners attempted the activity. However, when relatively brief written replies were called for, even when a grid, framework or space was provided, the response rate dropped dramatically to 30–50 per cent. These levels of response were similar to those detected when learners were asked to provide written responses and when no grid, framework or space was provided. Yet again the pattern of responses indicated by the three data collection methods were extremely similar.

Operational: the method of response required from a student

Throughout the teaching material students were invited to think critically about the ideas presented and were free to make whatever written notes they wished; in most cases this invitation was implicit. However, the practice of merely thinking about the answer rather than assembling a written response was common:

> … the ones that say 'jot down what your own feelings are about this'… I tend not, in fact, to jot down my feelings about it because I know I have got it up here and I don't generally need to commit those to paper… I vaguely know my own thoughts on things without putting them into words, without thinking too deeply.

> I always try at least to think about my answer to an activity.

The teaching material that was the focus of the investigation included several activities that actually recommended a form of mental or written response. Furthermore, the intellectual demands and typographical features of the tasks were similar – comprehension and recall with no grid, space or framework provided for a response. Between 70 and 90 per cent of students responded to those activities that called for a mental response. In contrast, only 30–50 per cent responded to those activities that called for a written response.

Within the teaching material there were other activities that also suggested mental responses and which did not provide a grid or framework for learner responses. However, their intellectual demands were greater, requiring interpretation and analysis. The proportion of learners responding to these activities varied but was amongst the lowest recorded in the entire study; ranging from 10 to 40 per cent.

There does appear to be a clear trend which, despite minor fluctuations, was reproduced in each of the data from interviews, tapes and questionnaires. Those activities demanding a mental response are much more likely to be completed than those demanding a written response. Indeed, the levels of response to the two parts of the same activity support this suggestion; the part of the activity that required a mental response being more than twice as likely to be completed than part of the same activity that required a written response. However, it must be stressed that the evidence is limited and, as earlier comments would suggest, the relative position of such activities may inflate the level of response, and the absence of a grid or framework for written replies may depress it.

A final indicator of a trend related to the intellectual operation required to complete activities was provided by a series of other activities that required demanding mental responses (interpretation and analysis) and which did not provide a framework or space for an answer. The levels of response for these activities, of between 10 and 40 per cent, were amongst the lowest recorded within material. The operation required of the student, mental or written, does appear to influence their level of response.

In order to respond to an activity, either mentally or in writing, a student must have read it. Indeed, evidence from interviews, tapes and questionnaires indicates that the textual material that constitutes an activity is invariably read even if the tasks posed are ignored. The proportion of students responding to those activities that had several parts illustrated this phenomenon; the first part of an activity completed by a large proportion of learners but only about half responding to the second part and even less to the third part. In other activities that had multiple parts a similar trend could be identified in data from the three collection methods.

Intellectual: the intellectual response required of a student

Comments from many students revealed a reluctance to engage with the more demanding intellectual activities compared to those demanding recall or comprehension. The following are typical of comments made in connection with more demanding activities:

> … I don't know if they're helpful or not. Sometimes I feel they get in the way. They make me think. I don't want to think, I just want to get on.

> … some of them were very good, very searching… I think if it were too searching it might be the thing that went.

> … this is the type of activity that I avoid… looks a bit complicated… no, that's too hard so I won't bother.

It was possible to differentiate between those activities in the material that demanded recall and comprehension and those that required higher level skills such as interpretation and analysis. However, previous discussion indicates that the Positional, Typographical and Operational features associated with activities influence students' response. As such any comparison of activities in terms of their intellectual features should attempt to mitigate their influence. A minority of the activities in the material provided a framework or grid within which to record a response – a feature that does appear to increase student response. When these activities were excluded from the comparison it was possible to identify four activities that required high level intellectual skills. Amongst these were three activities requiring a mental response and two a written response.

An analysis of the data indicated a much higher level of response for activities requiring recall and comprehension than for interpretation and analysis.

Temporal: the time officially allocated to an activity

While remarks on available study time pervaded student comments, only a small proportion made any reference to the specific time allowance that was allocated to an activity. The comments that were made were extremely varied and there was no detectable trend in terms of responses according to the time allocated to an activity. For example, isolated students maintained that their response to an activity was not influenced by the time allocation at all:

> The time allocation … is of little relevance … you can't avoid it because it is right next to the activity but I don't honestly think that has any real relevance.

> I'm not guided by the amount of time it says either because I find throughout the OU courses the timings are unreal ... so I tend to [ignore them] and spend as much time as I think is useful.

Others remarked that the time indicated did exert an influence on their response:

> ... the time allocation that they allow you is probably the deciding factor for me.

> ... if they are five minute ones I do them, but if they are fifteen or twenty minutes then I [do not].

> If I analysed the ones that I have done it is the shorter ones rather than the longer ones.

Any analysis is further complicated by the knowledge that some of the times allocated to activities were underestimates as acknowledged by writers. Several students also expressed doubts about the times allocated to activities:

> One of them in [the teaching material] was a 30 minute suggestion. I mean, it could have taken a day, two days.

> ... it says how much time you are allowed for it, but I think sometimes that's not completely accurate if you get over-involved.

Future research may be able to investigate whether the time allocated to an activity does influence student response to them.

Concluding comments

The five features that were identified – Temporal, Positional, Typographical, Operational and Intellectual – are each associated with a trend in student use of activities, the effects of which are compounded, and which appear to both support and influence learners' operation of the cost-benefit analysis model.

The response of learners to early activities in the material did appear to be greater than for subsequent ones. There was a tendency to either degrade or ignore the latter activities in each part of the teaching text in an attempt to save time or maintain the study schedule. In this context the effect of writers burying activities in the text and underestimating the time demands was counter-productive. It increased rather than reduced study time pressures and resulted in feelings of guilt and inadequacy as a result of their actions rather than feelings of being an effective and efficient learner. The provision of a framework, grid or space within an activity did appear to promote an increased response, their absence to depress it. For example, although one learner resolved the conflict between the benefits offered by activities and the costs by virtually ignoring them she found herself filling in a grid as part of an activity:

> There was a little grid and you had to add things… I just remember writing things in boxes and I was quite surprised with myself because I've never done that before.

These findings are consistent with those reported in other OU studies, (Henderson, 1977). The level of response for those activities requiring mental response rather than written one was also evident. This, in itself, need not cause undue concern. However, the fleeting nature of these mental responses, coupled with a higher response rate for those activities involving recall and comprehension compared to those involving interpretation and analysis does. Furthermore, the extent to which learners degrade activities and display deference to writers' comments is in contrast to authors' intentions of providing opportunities for students to think and engage with the material.

Chapter 5

Where do we go from here?

Guidelines for the design of activities

I'm in a dilemma. *(Sounds like the start of a dialogue doesn't it – it could be, but I'll continue with the style I've adopted throughout the book so far.)* On the one hand I do not believe there is a simple recipe for the design of activities – one that will work every time if you simply follow the instructions. On the other hand, I think within the evidence, examples and discussion presented in the previous chapters there is a series of features that are likely to contribute to better communication between you and your learners and to the teaching effectiveness of any activities you design. I ought to say here that I am *not* talking about the academic quality or technical accuracy of material in an activity. Indeed, I am making a distinction between teaching effectiveness and academic quality or technical accuracy. For example, I would argue that it would be possible to take completely false information and design an activity that would teach it effectively; the features of academic quality are not the same as those for teaching effectiveness. While I can comment upon those features that I feel contribute towards the teaching effectiveness of an activity, I will have to leave its academic quality or technical accuracy up to you.

However, I'm also aware of the criticisms that have been levelled at educational technologists who have adopted a mechanical approach to the design of self-instructional materials – even coining the term 'instructional industrialism' to describe it (Evans and Nation, 1989b). I trust that you will regard the comments in this section as a series of guidelines for you to consider, not a prescription for you to follow. Activity 5.1, which is of the tutorial-in-print and reflective action guide type, is an opportunity for you to identify those features that I have tried to incorporate into each of my activities and to decide the extent to which you feel they are worthwhile.

ACTIVITY 5.1 Guidelines for the design of activities

In the book so far I have provided 13 activities; this is the fourteenth, in which I have tried to incorporate those features that various educationalists and researchers believe will enhance the teaching effectiveness of activities. In fact I have already started to incorporate some of these features in this activity!

If you and your colleagues will be designing activities for inclusion in self-instructional texts at some time in the future I think 20 minutes or so trying to

1. identify those features, embodied in the various activities, that contribute to their teaching effectiveness;

2. compare your list of features with mine and consider their respective merits; and

3. design an activity which incorporates these features into an activity of your choice or check their presence in an activity you have readily available

would be a worthwhile use of your time.

1. Identify features embodied in the various activities

The discussion in Chapter 4 will have alerted you to the Positional, Typographical, Operational, Intellectual and Temporal features that learners associate with activities. This could be your starting point in identifying those features embodied in the present and the previous 13 activities. I think you would find it useful to spend five minutes looking through each of the activities I have provided and trying to identify what these are. You can list them in the space below.

So what features did you identify? If you used those in Chapter 4 as a guide I'm pretty sure you noted that the activities have been a regular feature of the book – distributed fairly evenly throughout. You probably also noted that, in general, an activity has been posed on each key aspect of the content, like this sub-section on identifying the guidelines, and that I have tried to identify them typographically by placing the Activity within a box, typing in the word 'activity', its number and title. I've also tried to provide a space or grid for your response. You may have noted that I I been asking you to do a variety of things, from thinking about your attitudes, beliefs and assumptions, consulting/reviewing other material, talking with colleagues, to making a written record and drafting activities – in fact a whole range of cognitive activities. I'm also sure you noted that in each case I've given you an indication of the amount of time that I think the activity deserves. However, these are not the only features that characterize the series of activities; let me take one activity as an example and describe what I mean.

In Figure 5.1 I have reproduced Activity 3.1 but superimposed a series of marginal notes; those features that each of the activities typically contain. If you turn back to page 70, you will note that it had a *SUBHEADING* for the section in which the activity occurs; the subsequent textual material provides the *CONTEXT* for the activity. In Figure 5.1 I have put these marginal notes before the activity. The activity itself has a *TITLE*. Immediately after the *TITLE* the activity is introduced and a *RATIONALE* provided as to why it is worth time and effort to respond. A rationale is vital. If you cannot think of a good reason why it is worth posing the activity perhaps it isn't worth posing at all! Trivial activities get the treatment they deserve from learners; they are skipped. Unfortunately the effect is that often subsequent activities, that may be worthwhile, receive the same cursory treatment as trivial ones. You may recall the comment of the student in Chapter 3 who appeared to have got into the habit of not doing the activities regardless of their possible merits. I have already mentioned the *TYPOGRAPHICAL* features associated with the activities. You will undoubtedly have noticed in Examples 1.1 to 1.11 that a variety of other typographical features, symbols or icons have been used. The variety is enormous. In Example 1.1 alone you can see bold lines across the page, boxed comments, icons of a magnifying glass and of Big Ben. Other icons, like cassette tape symbols and quill pen and parchment (Example 1.2) are widely used. In each activity an indication of the *TIME* likely to be appropriate is also provided. Of course this can only be indicative. Different learners will bring different abilities, skills and interests to the material. An activity that would take one learner 5 minutes could take others 25 minutes. However, it does serve to give an indication of the order of magnitude, realizing of course that it is extremely unlikely that you will be able to structure and control how learners use your whole material, never mind an individual activity. Each activity also has a set of clear *INSTRUCTIONS* usually followed by an *EXAMPLE* and a *SPACE OR GRID* for the learners' subsequent response. Finally I trust you recognized that each of the activities was accompanied by *FEEDBACK* or follow up comments.

Many of the examples provided in the previous chapters embody several of these features. For example, the one drawn from the National Association of Clinical Tutors Training Package, Example 1.12, contains a subheading for the activity, the first paragraph of text provides a context for it and the second paragraph a rationale for its inclusion. The typographical layout and bold rules across the page flag the presence of the activity as well as indicating the approximate study time that may be required to complete it. Simple instructions precede a framework or response space whilst the final two paragraphs provide the learner with feedback.

2. Compare your list of features with mine and consider their merits

Did you identify similar features to the ones listed and described above? If you did, do you accept that they are likely to contribute to the teaching effectiveness of your activities? If not, what other features did you identify and how would you judge their merits?

One feature that I would like to think also runs through each of the activities I have posed and contributes to the teaching effectiveness of them is the language. I have tried to adopt an informal tone and style that simulates the 'implied dialogue' mentioned in Chapter 1. You will have to judge if this writing style has been clear and simple, if technical terms and jargon have been avoided, if the speed and tone of the writing has been appropriate to you. You may find, like me and many of my colleagues, that it is all too easy to revert to the 'academic' or 'scholarly' style more appropriate to a journal article or technical presentation, which would be inappropriate for a self-instructional text.

Depending upon your reaction to the above comments I would suggest that a few minutes of your time could be well spent making a note of your comments and reactions in the space below. Unfortunately, I cannot know what other features, if any, you have identified nor your judgement as to their merits. However, I trust you will satisfy yourself about this possibility before continuing.

3. *Incorporate these features into an activity of your choice*

You will recall that activities 1.2 and 1.3 gave you the opportunity to begin the design of an activity of your choice; you may have taken up this opportunity. If you did you now have the chance to check the extent to which this activity, or any other one you may have designed or which is readily available, embodies the features that have been identified. It should take you only two to three minutes to determine if these features are in fact present – perhaps another 10 minutes or so to draft changes that would provide those that are missing.

Of course, you don't have to simply accept one set of features and discount others when designing your activities and deciding which guidelines are most appropriate. I imagine that during the process of writing your self-instructional material you will be trying out draft material with real learners and getting their comments and reaction to it. Certainly, the majority of providers of self-instructional material trial, pre-test or developmentally test their material (Henderson et al, 1983; Nathenson and Henderson, 1980) before it is printed and circulated for study. You have the opportunity to assess the impact of these features upon the teaching effectiveness of material with your learners before you commit yourself to print.

Figure 5.1 *Features of effective activities*

Writers' assumptions and expectations

ACTIVITY 3.1 Writers' assumptions and expectations

At this point I think you would find it useful to spend a couple of minutes trying to identify the assumptions that lie behind the self-instructional material that you currently assemble or are likely to assemble in the near future. In the space below you can note your main assumptions and alongside each of these you could note what your expectations are regarding the way in which your learners will study your material in general and the activities in particular.

(a) What assumptions lie behind the self-instructional materials you will be assembling and the activities you will be devising?

(b) What expectations do you have regarding the way in which learners will study your material in general and the activities in particular ?

Example:

ASSUMPTION
1. Activities are an integral part of teaching, a way to realize key objectives, with the rest of the material built around them.

EXPECTATION
Learners will recognize the central place of activities in their study since they provide an opportunity to realize and practise objectives.

2.

3.

4.

So what assumptions, and corresponding expectations, regarding activities and learner use did you identify? I obviously can't know which ones you have listed but I can share with you those listed by other teachers and writers. In surveys of OU authors and discussion with other writers of self-instructional material five major ones have emerged; I've summarized these in Figure 3.1. As I go through them perhaps you would like to consider how they compare with yours and whether you would adopt or reject them.

CONTEXT

SUBHEADING

TYPOGRAPHICAL
TITLE

TIME
RATIONALE

INSTRUCTIONS

EXAMPLE

SPACE OR GRID

FEEDBACK

Implications for writers and learners

It is likely that activities will remain a characteristic of self-instructional texts for the foreseeable future, be they of the tutorial-in-print, reflective action guide, dialogue type, some combination of these or a form yet to be suggested. It is also likely that you and your colleagues will spend considerable time and energy in designing them. As a result your review of the evidence and arguments presented so far, and the implications for you, your colleagues and your learners, is both necessary and timely.

It is inevitable when people start to review current practices and resultant materials that they talk about the evidence that can be assembled; it can sound very grand and scholarly. Of course isolated comments from colleagues, features in a particular activity and your own feelings are probably more like indicators than evidence. However, at the outset this is all you may have; you have to make your judgement as to whether you want to act on these indicators or collect evidence on a systematic basis.

In this context it occurs to me that the most appropriate form for a review would be an activity of the reflective action guide type. In such an activity I can provide guidelines and suggestions for the issues to be addressed but cannot anticipate the resultant outcome. The outcome would obviously be based upon your current practices and the extent to which you have accepted or rejected the points I have raised. It would really be up to you to conduct your own review, judge your practices, and existing materials and reach a decision regarding your future actions. I don't really think it could be anything else.

I also find it impossible to say how long this review is likely to take. It depends upon your reaction so far to the arguments and points I have presented, your response to the various activities I have offered and the extent to which you have talked to colleagues, reviewed existing material and reflected upon the current role of activities in your own teaching and within your own institution. However, I firmly believe that the time you spend will be well spent.

Activity 5.2 is offered as a framework for your review, to consider the implications of the issues I have raised for you and your learners.

Activity 5.2 Implications for writers and learners

I would suggest that the basis of your review is the content of Chapters 1 to 4. These provided the opportunity for you to consider those issues that I believe are of fundamental importance to those designing activities in texts and those responding to them. The Contents and List of activities provide a ready guide to the issues addressed and activities that were offered. I would suggest that in reviewing the evidence and arguments presented you look through the Contents and List of activities and consider the following questions.

- Can you identify and describe the espoused theories that you and your colleagues have regarding activities in texts and which you communicate to others – including your learners?
- Can you identify examples of the theories-in-use that you and your colleagues practise with regard to activities in texts that may be inconsistent with your espoused theories or even counter-productive?
- Do you and your colleagues share certain assumptions regarding activities and how learners will use them; if so what are they?
- Do you have any evidence (or indicators) of how your learners perceive and use activities and the extent to which these match your own expectations?
- Are you able to support, or challenge, the claim that learners recognize the benefits that activities provide and the costs that are incurred in responding to them; that they operate a cost-benefit analysis?
- Are there any other implications for you and your learners that should be addressed ?

I trust you found this a worthwhile if somewhat sobering activity. Sobering in that I suspect it may have revealed a number of practices that are neither in your interests nor those of your colleagues or learners. Sobering in that you may have discovered that you have extremely few indicators and little or no evidence from which to reach a decision.

I think the previous chapters reveal a disturbing picture concerning the production of activities by writers and their reception by learners; one that will, I hope, cause writers to reconsider the role of activities in their self-instructional material. I don't want to paraphrase the previous chapters but rather to remind you of some of the key issues that you will have to consider and resolve.

Have you been able to identify any differences between what you and your colleagues *say you do* regarding the design and integration of activities in self-instructional texts and what you and they *actually do*? Certainly, amongst many writers and within a variety of institutions, I have identified a mismatch between espoused theories and theories-in-use. If such a mismatch is present in your working context it needs to be revealed and resolved, since writers communicate espoused theories amongst themselves and to learners in course materials. This may be done in an introduction and guide and in preliminary comments but also in ways that permeate the entire teaching text. Have you detected the practices that I gave as examples – activities presented with unrealistic time allocations, or with unrealistic academic demands, or which are buried in the text – leaving learners with the dilemma as to whether to respond or not? The decision to respond to such activities providing worthwhile benefits but increasing the workload; the decision to skip over an activity obviously saving time but at what cost? Have you detected any indication of the cumulative effect of increased workload – to a level where learners start to incur intellectual and emotional costs to their learning? For some learners the effect can be dramatic and may result in a decision to withdraw from the course. Certainly, studies which sought to understand student drop-out and withdrawal from OU courses (Woodley, 1987; Woodley and Parlett, 1983) have repeatedly emphasized the adverse effect of excessive course workload on students' decisions to continue study and their method of studying.

Of course, you may not be the most popular colleague around if you do detect these differences, since people are likely to be unaware of them. However, if you regard the intellectual and emotional welfare of your learners to be of paramount importance you really have no choice.

The previous chapters have also revealed a mismatch between writers' assumptions and expectations regarding activities and learners' perceptions and use of them. I don't want to repeat the previous chapter but just to remind you of the common, but flawed assumption identified previously; that the task of the teacher is to carefully control how students learn. On the opening page of the article published by Rothkopf and Bloom, the same one used in Activity 2.2, the authors say that,

An important practical problem for self-instructional libraries is how to shape and sustain effective (mathemagenic) activities (Rothkopf and Bloom, 1970, p 417).

Others have perpetuated this assumption when they say that:

… the instructor aims to shape or channel these natural cognitive processes to ensure that the content presented… is acquired (Winne, 1983, p 243).

However, despite the studies I have already mentioned that indicate that even if the control of student learning was a desirable goal it would be impossible to achieve, researchers still report attempts by teachers to control and manipulate the way their learners use their self-instructional material (Marland et al, 1990). Is this an assumption that your colleagues still hold? If so it has major implications for the design of your activities.

The evidence and arguments that I presented suggest that both educational and emotional costs may be a product of course workload as students operate within a cost-benefit analysis model with regard to activities in texts. The study that I undertook indicated that a substantial proportion of learners became study time savers, they degraded activities and developed feelings of inadequacy. Furthermore, it indicated that learners invariably recognized the course-focused, self-focused and assignment-focused benefits provided by activities, but simply did not avail themselves of them. I obviously cannot know the extent to which your learners do or do not operate a cost-benefit analysis, but I trust you will consider the possibility and implications for your teaching.

Finally, were you able to identify any other implications for your colleagues and learners? Simply raising the above issues is one way of raising others.

References

Anderson, R C and Biddle, B W (1975) 'On asking people questions about what they are reading', in: Bower, G H (ed), *The Psychology of Learning and Motivation*, New York: Academic Press.

Andre, T (1987) 'Questions and learning from reading', *Questioning Exchange*, 1, 1, pp 47–86.

Argyris, C and Schön, D A (1974)*Theory in Practice. Increasing Professional Effectiveness*, San Francisco: Jossey-Bass.

Bloom, B S et al. (1956)*Taxonomy of Educational Objectives. Handbook I. Cognitive Domain*, London: Longman Green and Co.

Brighouse, A, Godber, D and Patilla, P (1987)*Calculator Book*, Walton-on-Thames: Thomas Nelson and Sons.

The British Soft Drinks Association Limited (1987) *Soft Drinks Today*, London: The British Soft Drinks Association Limited.

Brown, G (1978) *Lecturing and Explaining*, London: Methuen.

Cardiff University College (1986) *POPTRAN Program Guide 3. Population Projections for Selected Countries*, Cardiff: Cardiff University College Population Centre.

Carver, R P (1972) 'A critical view of mathemagenic behaviours and the effects of questions upon the retention of prose material', *Journal of Reading Behaviour*, 4, pp 93–119.

Central Planning Unit (1991)*The Road Traffic Act 1991: An Officers' Guide,* Harrogate: Central Planning Unit.

Crick, M (1980) 'Course teams: myth and actuality', *Distance Education*, 1, 2, pp 127–41.

Dahlgren, L O (1975) 'Qualitative differences in learning as a function of content-oriented guidance', *Göteborg Studies in Educational Sciences, No.15*, University of Göteborg.

Duchastel, P S (1979) 'Adjunct questions effect and experimental constraints', *The American College, Department of Research and Evaluation, Occasional Paper 1*, Bryn Mawr, Pennsylvania.

Duchastel, P S (1983) 'Interpreting adjunct question research: processes and ecological validity', *Human Learning*, **2**, pp 1–5.

Duchastel, P S and Whitehead, D (1980)'Exploring student reactions to inserted questions in texts', *Programme Learning and Educational Technology*, **17**, 1, pp 41–47.

Elzey, F F (1965) *A Programmed Introduction to STATISTICS*, Belmont: Wadworth Publishing Company.

Entwistle, N (1984) 'Contrasting perspectives on learning', in: Marton, F, Hounsell, D and Entwistle, N (eds), *The Experience of Learning*, Edinburgh: Scottish Academic Press.

Evans, T (1984) 'Communicating with students by audio tape', *Teaching at a Distance*, **25**, pp 108–10.

Evans, T (1989)'Fiddling while the tome turns: reflections of a distance education development consultant', in: Parer, M (ed), *Development, Design and Distance Education*, Churchill, Victoria: Centre for Distance Learning, Gippsland Institute of Advanced Education.

Evans, T (1991) 'An introduction to critical issues in distance education: I', in: Evans, T (ed), *Critical Issues in Distance Education*, Geelong: Deakin University Press.

Evans, T and Nation, D (1989a) 'Dialogue in practice, research and theory in distance education', *Open Learning*, **4**, 2, pp 37–42.

Evans T and Nation, D (1989b) 'Reflecting on the project', in: Evans, T and Nation, D (eds), *Critical Reflections on Distance Education*, London: Falmer Press.

Farrally, M (1991) *An Introduction to the Structure of the Body*, The National Coaching Foundation, Leeds, in conjunction with The Scottish Sports Council, Edinburgh.

Faw, H W and Waller, T G (1976) 'Mathemagenic behaviours and efficiency in learning from prose materials. Review, critique and recommendations', *Review of Educational Research*, **46**, 4, pp 691–720.

Fayol, M, (1987) 'Are there any surface cues that can help students select main points in texts? A tentative review', Paper presented at the Second European Conference for Research on Learning and Instruction, Tubingen, West Germany, September.

Frase, L T (1970) 'Boundary conditions for mathemagenic behaviours', *Review of Educational Research*, **40**, 3, pp 337–347.

Geotz, J P (1984) *Ethnography and Qualitative Design in Educational Research*, London: Academic.

Gibbs, G, Lockwood, F G, Morgan, A and Taylor, E (1982) 'Student learning and course design 1: In-text teaching devices in Open University texts', *Open University Institute of Educational Technology Study Methods Group Report 12*.

Giles, G and Evans, G (1991) *Compiling Written Records of Tape Recorded Interviews,* Birmingham: West Midlands Police Training Centre.

Gillard, G (1981) 'The implied teacher-student dialogue in distance education', in Crump, P and Livingstone, K (eds), *ASPESA FORUM '81.* Papers Supplementary Volume.

Goodwin, C (1991) *Operational Management,* London: Hotel Catering and Institutional Management Association.

Grantham College of Education (1989) *A Brief Introduction to Children's Development,* Hong Kong: Education Department.

Hamaker, C (1986) 'The effects of adjunct questions on prose learning', *Review of Educational Research,* **56,** 2, pp 212–42.

Hamilton, R J (1985) 'A framework for the evaluation of the effectiveness of adjunct questions and objectives', *Review of Educational Research,* **55,** 1, pp 47–85.

Harrow, A J (1972) *A Taxonomy of the Psychomotor Domain,* New York: David McKay Co.

Hartley, J (1985) *Designing Instructional Texts,* London: Kogan Page.

Henderson, E S (1977) 'Student response rates to questions in A101 Texts', Open University Institute of Educational Technology, (mimeo).

Henderson, E S *et al* (1983) 'Developmental testing for credit: a symposium', *Institutional Research Review,* **2,** pp 39–59.

Henderson, E S, Kinzett, S and Lockwood, F G (1988) 'Developing POPTRAN, a population modelling package', *British Journal of Educational Technology,* **19,** 3, pp 184–192.

Indira Gandhi National Open University (1991) *AFW – 1 Feature Writing,* Delhi: Indira Gandhi National Open University.

Inland Revenue (1991) *Husband and Wife: Joint Assets and Outgoings,* Liverpool: Open Learning Unit.

Jeffcote, R (1981) 'Why can't a unit be more like a book?', *Teaching at a Distance,* **20,** pp 75–76.

Kaikumba, N and Cryer, P (1987) 'Evaluating at a distance using cassette tape', *Open Learning,* **2,** pp 59–61.

Katholieke Universiteit Leuven (1992) *Inleiding tot de QUANTUM-MECHANICA,* Leuven: Apeldoorn Garant.

Kaye, A (1972) 'Students' use of course materials', Open University Institute of Educational Technology, (mimeo).

Knapper, C (1980)*Evaluating Instructional Technology,* Beckenham: Croom Helm.

Krathwohl, D R, Bloom, B S and Masia, B B (1964)*Taxonomy of Educational Objectives: Affective Domain,* London: Longman.

Laurillard, D M (1978) 'A study of the relationship between some of the cognitive and contextual factors in student learning', unpublished PhD thesis, University of Surrey.

Lawless, C J (1976) 'An investigation of students' responses to questions in AMST283, Unit 11, "Genesis and Geology"', Open University Institute of Educational Technology, (mimeo).

Lockwood, F G (1989a) 'The evaluation of Open University preparatory packages', *Open Learning*, **4** 2, pp 43–6.

Lockwood, F G (1989b) 'A course developer in action – a reassessment of activities in texts', in: Parer, M (ed), *Development, Design and Distance Education*, Churchill, Victoria: Centre for Distance Learning, Gippsland Institute of Advanced Education.

Lockwood, F G (1989c) 'Data collected by self recorded audio cassette tape', *Research in Distance Education*, **1**, 2, pp 7–8.

Lockwood, F G (1990) 'Activities in distance learning texts', unpublished PhD thesis, Open University.

Lockwood, F G (1992) 'Alternative methods of materials production', *Media and Technology for Human Resource Development*.

MacDonald-Ross, M (1970) 'Notes on objectives, assessment and activities', Open University Institute of Educational Technology, (mimeo).

Mager, R F (1990)*Preparing Instructional Objectives*, London: Kogan Page.

Marland, P (1989) 'An approach to research on distance learning', *British Journal of Educational Technology* **20**, 3, pp 173–82.

Marland, P *et al* (1990) 'Distance learners' interactions with text while studying', *Distance Education*, **11**, 1, pp 71–91.

Marton, F (1975) 'On non-verbatim learning II. The erosion effect of a task-induced learning alogorithm', *Report from the Institute of Education, No.40,* University of Göteburg.

Marton, F (1981) 'Phenomenography – describing conceptions of the world around us', *Instructional Science*, **10**, pp 177–200.

Marton, F and Säljö, R (1976) 'On qualitative differences in learning, I – outcome as a function of the learners' conception of the task', *British Journal of Educational Psychology,* **46**, pp 115–27.

Marton, F and Svensson, L (1980) 'Conceptions of research in student learning', *Higher Education*, **9**, pp 39–51.

Mathias, H S (1980) 'Science students' approaches to learning', *Higher Education*, **9**, pp 39–51.

The Medicine Group (1991) *Seeking Standards in Practice. Coronary Heart Disease Prevention Programmes*, Abingdon, Oxon: The Medicine Group.

Midland Examining Group (1990) *Geography Syllabus A. General Certificate of Secondary Education Examination Syllabuses*, Midland Examining Group.

Miller, C M L and Parlett, M (1974)*Up to the Mark. A Study of the Examination Game*, Society for Research in Higher Education, Monograph 21.

Misanchuk, E R (1992) *Preparing Instructional Texts*, New Jersey: Educational Technology Publications.

Modra, H M (1991) 'On the possibility of dialogue in distance education: a dialogue', in: Evans, T and King, B (eds), *Beyond the Text: Contemporary Writing on Distance Education*, Geelong: Deakin University Press.

Morgan, A (1987) 'Project work in open learning', in: Thorpe, M and Grugeon, D (eds), *Open Learning for Adults*, London: Longmans.

Morgan, A, Gibbs, G and Taylor, E (1980) 'The work of the study methods group', *Open University Institute of Educational Technology Study Methods Group Report No.1.*

Morgan, A, Gibbs, G and Taylor, E (1981) 'What do Open University students initially understand about learning?', *Open University Institute of Educational Technology, Study Methods Group Report 8.*

Moser, C A (1971) *Survey Methods in Social Investigation*, London: Heinemann.

Mulkay, M (1985) *The Word and the World: Explorations in the Form of Sociological Analysis*, London: Allen and Unwin.

Nathenson, M B (1978) 'Bridging the gap between teaching and learning at a distance', *British Journal of Educational Technology,* 10, pp 100–109.

Nathenson, M B and Henderson, E S (1980) *Using Student Feedback to Improve Learning Materials*, Beckenham: Croom Helm.

Nation, D (1991) 'Teaching texts and independent learning', in: Evans, T and King, B (eds), *Beyond the Text: Contemporary Writing on Distance Education*, Geelong: Deakin University Press.

National Association of Clinical Tutors (1990) *NACT Training Package*, NACT, London.

Nicodemus, R (1992) 'Understanding course teams: organisation and dynamics', *Open University Institute of Educational Technology, Teaching and Consultancy Centre Report 62.*

Nunan, T (1991)*An Introduction to Research Paradigms in Distance Education*, Geelong: Deakin University Press.

Open University (1979a) *T4101: Technology Project Course*, Milton Keynes: Open University Press.

Open University (1979b) *Science: A Foundation Course, Unit 14, Chemical Equilibrium*, Milton Keynes: Open University Press.

Open University (1981) *E200 Contemporary Issues in Education, Unit 10, Control and Choice in the School*, Milton Keynes: Open University Press.

Open University (1982)*A403: Arts and Society in British Society since the Thirties*, Milton Keynes: Open University Press.

Open University (1984) *Course Production Handbook*, Milton Keynes: Open University Press.

Open University (1985a) *Making Self-instructional Material for Adults*, Milton Keynes: Open University Press.

Open University (1985b) *Preparing for the Mathematics Foundation Course*, Milton Keynes: Open University Press.

Open University (1990) *M101 and MS283 Diagnostic Quiz*, Milton Keynes: Open University Press.

Open University (1992) *A214 Understanding Music: Elements, Techniques and Styles, Unit 4, Melody*, Milton Keynes: Open University Press.

Parlett, M and Hamilton, D (1977) 'Evaluation as illumination: a new approach to the study of innovatory programs', in: Hamilton, D *et al* (eds), *Beyond the numbers game*, Basingstoke: Macmillan.

Perry, W (1976) *Open University. A Personal Account by the First Vice-chancellor*, Milton Keynes: Open University Press.

Perry, W G (1970) *Forms of Intellectual and Ethical Development in College Years: A Scheme*, New York: Holt, Rinehart and Winston.

Reid, I (1982) 'Beyond English and the classroom', in: Mallick, D *et al*, (eds), *New Essays in the Teaching of Literature*, Norwood: Australian Association for Teaching English.

Rickards, J P and Denner, P R (1978) 'Inserted questions as aids to reading text', *Instructional Science*, 7, pp 313–46.

Riley, J (1983) 'The preparation of teaching in higher education', unpublished PhD thesis, University of Sussex.

Rothkopf, E Z (1965) 'Some theoretical and experimental approaches to problems in written instruction', in: Krumboltz, J D (ed), *Learning and the Educational Process*, New York: Rand McNally.

Rothkopf, E Z (1970) 'The concept of mathemagenic activities', *Review of Educational Research*, 40, 3, pp 325–35.

Rothkopf, E Z and Bloom, R D (1970) 'Effect of interpersonal interaction on the instructional value of adjunct questions in learning from written material', *Journal of Educational Psychology*, 61, 6, pp 417–22.

Rowntree, D (1973) 'Student exercises in correspondence texts', Open University, Institute of Educational Technology, (mimeo).

Rowntree, D (1974) *Educational Technology in Curriculum Development*, London: Harper and Row.

Rowntree, D (1975) 'Two styles of communication and their implications for learning', in: Baggaley, J, Jamieson, G H and Marchant, H (eds), *Aspects of Educational Technology VIII*, London: Pitman.

Rowntree, D (1979) 'Writing your lesson', in: Rowntree, D and Connors, B (eds), *How to Develop Self Instructional Teaching*, Milton Keynes: Open University Press.

Rowntree, D (1985) *Developing Courses for Students*, London: Harper and Row.

Rowntree, D (1990) *Teaching Through Self-Instruction*, London: Kogan Page.

Rowntree, D (1992) *Exploring Open and Distance Learning*, London: Kogan Page.

Säljö, R (1979a) 'Learning about learning', *Higher Education*, **80**, pp 443–51.

Säljö, R (1979b) 'Learning in the learners perspective I: Some common sense conceptions', *Reports from the Institute of Education University of Göteburg, No 76*.

Sanders, N M (1966)*Classroom Questions*, New York: Harper and Row.

Schumacher, G M and Young, D (1982) 'The effect of inserted questions on studying processes in normal textbook materials', Ohio State University (mimeo).

Science Museum (1991)*Flight Lab*, Science Museum, London.

Scottish Police College and National Computing Centre (1991) *Crowd Control: A Computer Based Training Exercise*, Tulliailan Castle, Kincardine: SPC.

Song, S Y, Park, S R and Kim, Y S (1991)*Introduction to Natural Science*, Seoul: Korea Air and Correspondence University.

South African Committee of Higher Education (1988) *Dawn Second Avenue*, Johannesburg: SACHED/Ravon.

Stringer, M (1980) 'Lifting the course team curse', *Teaching at a Distance*, **18**, pp 13–16.

Sukhothai Thammathirat Open University (1990) *English Language*, Bangpood: STOU Press.

Thunhurst, A (1990) *Front of House Operation*, London: Macmillan Education.

Winne, P H (1983) 'Training students to process text with adjunct aids', *Instructional Science*, **12**, pp 243–266, 1983.

Wong, B Y L (1985) 'Self-questioning instructional research: a review', *Review of Educational Research*, **55**, 2, pp 227–268.

Woodley, A (1987) 'Understanding adult student drop out', in: Thorpe, M and Grugeon, D (eds), *Open Learning for Adults*, London: Longmans.

Woodley, A and Parlett, M (1983) 'Student drop-out', *Teaching at a Distance*, **24** pp 2–23.